The Care & Feeding
of an
ATHLETE

By Toni Tickel Branner, MA

Care & Feeding of an Athlete

Published by Blue Water Press
Waxhaw, North Carolina

©Copyright 2007 by Blue Water Press
All Rights Reserved.

First Printing September 2007
Library of Congress Control Number: 2007935844
ISBN: 978-0-9796045-1-4

Cover design – Frank Rivera
Illustrations – Frank Foster
Interior design and layout – 1106 Design

Printed in Canada.

A book cannot replace personal guidance from a physician, registered
dietitian, or trained exercise professional. The advice in this book
includes general information based on research and is not designed to
treat any specific disease or condition.

The desire to win is born in most of us.
The will to win is a matter of training.
The manner of winning is a matter of honour.

—Margaret Thatcher

Table of Contents

Foreword

By Paul R. Stricker, MD
Sports Medicine Pediatrician and Olympic Physician
Author of *Sports Success Rx! —Your Child's Prescription for the Best Experience*

As a sports medicine pediatrician, I have found that many young athletes are eager to learn about their sport, improve their technique, find the best coach, and have the newest equipment to help their performance. Many of them utilize all of these tools and achieve some benefit. Many of them realize they need something more—something profound. Those who understand the value of good nutrition often hit the jackpot since the body can have all the training tools in the world, but be unable to perform without excellent nutrients to supply the body's exercise demands.

I was honored when Toni Branner asked me to contribute the Foreword to her *The Care & Feeding of an Athlete.* Her personal experience, knowledge, and commitment to the health of young people is exemplary, and a wonderful model of how to support our children's health without compromise. The information she provides should be used as tools upon which to build a great framework of performance benefits. Although the secret of whole food nutrition is not rocket science, its simplicity is also not a quick fix. Sound nutritional habits for the family will not only provide for the current exercise and school needs, but also provide for the long-term health and well-being of your children.

Years ago, it was known how carbohydrates provided useful energy for exercise. Later, science taught us the vital importance of replenishing carbohydrate stores quickly after intense exercise. More recently, research has exposed another important aspect of exercise and sports performance we must control—oxidative stress. Being able to neutralize harmful chemicals produced with exercise and emotional stress is accomplished with the powerful nutrients in fruits and vegetables. Mothers have been telling us this for years, but now we know a lot more about why certain foods offer so much to the long-term health of our bodies.

Toni's books offer much more than nutritional help—they emphasize that nutrition is just part of the overall picture. Fluids are immensely important, and a well-hydrated athlete is ready for optimal performance. Physical training, adequate rest, and emotional stamina are all required. Supporting your child without pressure is critical, and I appreciate the many aspects of the sports experience that are covered in these pages. Understanding all of the factors that go into sports activities is the first step to a successful outcome.

Approaching sports and exercise as a family is a great analogy to the "team" on which your young athletes participate. You are all in this together! Everyone can contribute to better health of the family, whether everyone is involved in sports or not. So be a team player and enjoy what reading lies ahead.

> If I can teach anything to my kids that I teach, it is to take care of their bodies. To feed and strengthen what God gave us to work with is vital to success. I see a lack of overall mental and physical strength in kids today and it saddens me. They are not conditioned like they should be. We are athletes and therefore must care for our bodies in that manner.
>
> —Caroline Lewis, Certified Personal Trainer,
> Professional Dancer, Choreographer

Athletes are often undernourished, although many of them eat lots of food. They often engage in eating patterns that may provide short-term benefits, but are unhealthy in the long-term. Fortunately, it is possible to enhance sports performance while building, not destroying health.

—Pamela A. Popper, PhD, ND
From *The Wellness Forum's Guide to Sports Nutrition*

Acknowledgements

I would like to thank the advisors and contributors who helped us with this book. First is my husband, Billy, who is the perfect example of a supportive, but not pushy parent of young athletes. Thank you to my children, Jenna and Will, who take on any sport or endeavor with enthusiasm and true commitment. I am proud of their leadership and work ethic on their athletic teams. My mother, Becky Brown, taught me about nutrition and the importance of muscle balance and core strength many years before personal trainers and coaches studied them.

Thank you to the many incredible coaches, parents, educators, and athletes who offered encouragement, support, and the opportunity to allow me and my colleagues to get this information to student athletes and their parents.

Thank you, too, to the health professionals who have the courage to teach what we really have to do to prevent disease and achieve optimal health. Just choosing the small fries instead of the large is not enough. This book introduces the newest state of the art research on optimal performance and on preventing disease in the future. Proper physical training can help all athletes, and although a plant-based diet may seem strange, it is not as hard as it seems. The research is very clear, and even very young athletes can understand concepts like oxidative stress and free radical damage.

—Sincerely,
Toni Tickel Branner, MA
Exercise Physiologist and Wellness Consultant

Board of Advisors and Contributors:

Charee Boulter, PhD
Licensed psychologist specializing in eating disorders, performance enhancement, substance abuse prevention, stress management, and mindfulness meditation.

William A. Branner, III, MD
Physician, Sports Dad, Proofreader.

Tina Marie Mendieta, MS, RD/LDN
Registered dietitian, fitness instructor, and wellness consultant.

Pam Popper, PhD, ND
Naturopathic Physician, Nutritionist, Owner of The Wellness Forum.

Paul Stricker, MD, FAAP
Sports Medicine Pediatrician and Olympic Physician, Past President of the American Medical Society for Sports Medicine
American Academy of Pediatrics Sports Medicine Council
Consultant for USA Swimming
Author of *Sports Success Rx!—Your Child's Prescription for the Best Experience.*

It doesn't take an arms inspector to spot one of the
biggest weapons of mass destruction facing Americans
today: It's the school lunch—full of saturated fat,
cholesterol and sugar, and devoid of any real nutrition.
The acronym for the Standard American Diet is very SAD
indeed. We are, SADly, overfed but undernourished.

—Susan Silberstein, PhD, from her book *Hungry for Health*
Director of the Center for Advancement in
Cancer Education, www.beatcancer.org

Introduction

This book came to be for several reasons. In my twenty years as an exercise physiologist, I have spent many hours teaching seminars and training coaches, athletes, corporate executives, senior citizens, and others who want to improve their performance and prevent disease. I have also spent many hours working with the parents of athletes. As parents, we take our job very seriously. We require the best car seats, regular dental care, and yearly physical check ups. We emphasize the importance of education and study habits so our children can learn how to make a successful life for themselves. We all want to do the right thing but sometimes it isn't clear which path is the correct choice. The United States and other developed nations are experiencing an epidemic of diabetes, obesity, asthma and other diseases in children. It is easier to "follow the herd" to fast food restaurants and send processed convenience foods in the lunchbox. It is easier and more acceptable to take Oreos® and soda to the after-game celebration than to take water, whole-grain bagels, and fruit.

In order to give our children a chance for a healthy future we have to jump back on a path of prevention. The research is very clear. The solution is simple but not always easy. We know exactly what we need to do to maximize athletic performance, optimize healthy growth in young people, and prevent long-term disease. The good news is that the exact same changes that improve sports performance will also improve focus and memory, lower the risk of cancer and heart disease, reduce the chance of developing eye disease and much more. There is no separate diet or health plan for all of these results. It is exactly the same plan. This book is designed to give the athlete and the athlete's family the tools to actually put this knowledge into practice.

As I attend games and sporting events, I notice how hard these young people are working but also how poorly they are taking care of themselves. Athletes train for hours in the gym and on the field and push themselves to high levels during competition. They deserve the same attention and education about nutrition, muscle care, and sports psychology, as the elite professional athletes receive.

As a sports family we have also learned much about how to make this time investment and financial commitment to athletics work for us in a positive way. Sharing these tips and techniques as well as sharing mistakes we have made along the way may save you some trouble and propel your family forward toward a beneficial and fun experience.

This book is for all types of athletes but especially for those who would like to move up to the next level. Beginners, travel team, college bound athletes, or "I'm doing this just for fun" participants will all benefit from the practical advice and strategies. It doesn't matter if you plan or hope to be a professional athlete. All of the advice in this book will help you grow up to be a healthy and successful adult. Although my husband and I were never professional athletes after college, we were able to accomplish many things in life because of the skills gained through sports. I was a college cheerleader and was able to travel around the country and the world with the University of North Carolina Chapel Hill teams. I know how to organize my time and juggle many projects at once. This is exactly what I had to do with school, chores, and practice when I was a student. I then became the owner of my own company and a professional speaker. I have no problem standing in front of a thousand people to teach a seminar and I owe this to the confidence and performance experience I gained through athletics.

What makes the information in *The Care & Feeding* series of books different from most books on this topic? The most important advantage is that the nutrition and physical training guidelines are based on state of the art research. You want to be healthy now and improve your performance now, but the approach in this book not only gives you the immediate benefits today but leads you into a lifetime of optimal health. We are just now starting to understand how important a plant-based diet is to current and long-term health and disease prevention. We are just starting to realize that there is no magic pill or supplement that will improve performance and health. It is the total diet—foods working together—that gives the body everything it needs to do its job. It is getting enough rest, training for speed, endurance, agility, and power. It is learning to think positively and focus on success. Starting an athlete on this road at a young age means they will deal with success in life, less illness, less disease, and fewer problems with weight control than the generation before them. Other topics, like reducing dairy consumption, consuming less animal protein, and consuming the recommended daily phytonutrients (from fruits and vegetables) are concepts that are incorporated into the suggestions for healthy eating. Preventing injuries by utilizing proper warm-up and physical training techniques are often neglected areas of education for the young athlete and are explained in these pages. The challenge for athletes and parents is to study these concepts together and then utilize the recommended resources to continue to learn about wellness and discuss these topics as a family.

You, the sports lover and dedicated athlete, are the inspiration for *The Care & Feeding of an Athlete*. So, get comfortable, take a few minutes to relax and start reading!

1. Sports: The Good, The Bad, and the Ugly

It is important to be passionate about something in your life. It might be art or video games or singing. This book is designed to support and encourage individuals who are passionate about a sport or sports in general. Whatever your reason for playing or competing, this book can help you reach the next level of achievement.

> From the beginning I loved it. Who knows why? It was just everything to me. I couldn't get enough of it. Tennis, tennis, tennis every day.
>
> —Monica Seles

> I always loved running—it was something you could do by yourself, and under your own power. You could go in any direction, fast or slow as you wanted, fighting the wind if you felt like it, seeking out new sights just on the strength of your feet and the courage of your lungs.
>
> —Jesse Owens

> Winning doesn't always mean being first. Winning means you're doing better than you've ever done before.
>
> —Bonnie Blair

Let's start by going over all of the positives. Many people just love to compete. It is fun to set goals and satisfying to work hard to accomplish them. When you win you can bask in the feeling of accomplishment. When you lose, you can set your sights on new techniques that will make a difference the next time. The important thing is to focus on the process and not the outcome. Win or lose, did you learn something and progress in your skills and knowledge of strategy?

In today's society of couch potatoes and video addicts, playing sports can be the answer for giving your body the exercise and physical conditioning necessary to maintain your health and to live life to the fullest. You will look better and feel better about yourself. You will have energy to do the mandatory things in your schedule with extra stamina for the fun stuff.

The relationships you build with teammates and coaches are invaluable. Friendships and shared memories are the first things that older athletes talk about when looking back on their middle school, high school and college sport experiences. You will develop camaraderie with your own teammates, other athletes at your school or travel team, rivals on other teams, fellow sport campers, and the families of these friends.

Today, traveling is a part of most athletic schedules. Whether it is the town one hour away or an event in another state or country, you will develop many social and life skills on these trips. You will meet other athletes with the same drive and focus that you have. In many situations you will see them season after season at the same events. If you go without your parents you will have to exhibit ethical behavior, learn to manage your meals and finances, and practice self-responsibility.

Athletes have a unique ability to have fun no matter how dire the circumstances. Playing in the rain and mud, dealing with extreme heat, and learning not to take a demanding coach too personally will all come in handy in later life. Athletes also develop a higher tolerance for fatigue and pain. This can be good and bad. You want to be able to push yourself but you should also recognize when the possibility of injury exists.

Athletes need to learn how important it is to take care of their body and health with good nutrition and muscle care. My kids have learned that it takes a lot of planning to do as much as they do without getting run down and sick. It takes effort to pack snacks and a cooler of water before practice. You'll have to get over it when the kids at school tease you about how different your lunch looks compared to their burger and fries. Some of them might even sample and like new, healthier foods because of you. Just a simple thing like making sure you are hydrated, will improve your athletic ability and your focus and performance on the field and at school. You don't get a new body when you get older so now is your chance to learn about healthy eating, warming up, proper training techniques, and stress management.

Occasionally you are faced with some experiences that are not so positive when you participate in sports: unsafe equipment and facilities, coaches who mean well but may not be well trained; a program where the competition is too easy or too hard can increase the chance that injuries will occur and decrease morale on the team. Programs that focus too much on winning and not enough on the skills of individual athletes and the team are detrimental, as are over-zealous parents who act inappropriately or place excessive pressure on their children and the coaches. In the ugliest of circumstances we have seen parents and spectators who boo the other team and yell at referees.

As an athlete, you learn how to push yourself to your fullest potential, learn to take criticism as a compliment, and learn to gain confidence from each experience. You feel pain, you experience success, you deal with defeat, and you gain irreplaceable friendships with other athletes. You have something to fall back on when everything else in your life is going wrong. The skills you learn through sports will never leave you.

A friend just sent me a quick note. She is a life long friend who is very athletic and has a son who is finishing a competitive collegiate soccer career. She said that she 'hoped my team was playing well because in the end that is really what matters the most, playing well and being good sports' (and don't let anyone fool you that it is all about winning). She finished by saying, 'That's from one jock to another.'

For me, this hits the nail on the head. Sure we all like to win, but the journey is all about doing your best to play well, about handling winning and loosing with grace and dignity. During the competitive moment, we strive to be the best we can in an effort to win but once the last whistle sounds or final point is played, that competition is over and the joy of the experience is what really matters. My hope, as a coach, is that in every game my team plays, they work as hard as they can individually and as a team and that ultimately they have fun playing together. Once the game is complete we reflect and learn from the experience. We gain insight and prepare for the next opportunity to compete.

This is a great life lesson for young men and women. We need to try as hard as we can in everything we do; sometimes we win and sometimes we are not so successful.

These successes and failures may be in academics with the grades we receive, in the job market as a finalist for a position, or in business with an account we are pursuing, but either way, we carry on in life, and learn from the experience so next time we improve our game. Life is about the journey— play well and value what we learn along the way.

—Dick Sipperly, collegiate and high school lacrosse player, educator, and varsity lacrosse coach at Charlotte Latin School

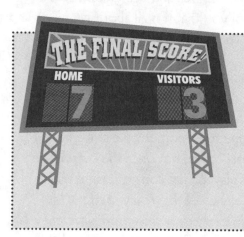

With hard work, a positive attitude, good training, and the right nutrition, you can rise to your fullest potential as an athlete!

2. Developing the Total Athlete

It was once thought that athletes did not need to take time to work on skill training, outside of playing time and regular work. Today, the world of sports is so physical and competitive that it is now expected that athletes should train for endurance, power, strength, agility and flexibility in addition to sport-specific activities. Even young athletes will benefit from extra physical training if safety and form are the priority. Prevention of injuries and muscle balance are two of the best reasons to add strength training, core exercises, and focused flexibility to the athlete's regimen. Starting these programs or fine-tuning what you are already doing will help you move up the ladder to the next level.

Let's take a look at the various components of a "fit" athlete.

Cardiovascular Endurance (Aerobic Fitness)

The word aerobic means "with oxygen." Oxygen is necessary to burn the fuels, which produce energy for prolonged activity. By exercising aerobically we initiate physiologic changes, which increase the efficiency of the heart, lungs, and circulatory system. A healthy heart has the ability to supply plenty of oxygen and nutrients to the working muscles during normal activities and sports movement, as well as any emergency situations that might arise. During a two-hour game or practice, it is important that your last play or run to be as great as your first. Athletes with aerobic endurance will not falter when they need to make the last second shot or to get to the other end of the field in time to make a play.

Aerobic activities are those that are rhythmical, continuous, and involve large muscle groups. Aerobic activities such as walking, running, cycling, swimming, and aerobic dance increase the heart rate to a target level and maintain it at that level for a certain length of time. Some athletic programs incorporate aerobic conditioning into their classes and some do not. You may need to add in your own aerobic conditioning or consult with a personal trainer if you need to supplement your training. In order to get a training effect, you must do regular aerobic activity. It does not help to do a nice jog every couple of weeks. Three-to-four workouts a week for 30 to 45 minutes are the minimum to maintain aerobic conditioning. Sometimes this is all you have time for and that's okay. During off weeks, during the summer, or on vacation you could add a few more days. If you are trying to control your weight, going for extra walks or jogs will make a difference. Your coach might incorporate this training into your practice by keeping you moving (keeping your heart rate elevated) the entire time with skills, sprints, and runs. This can be very effective because it is specific aerobic training for your sport.

Special Note: With any high impact activities like running, jumping rope, or aerobic dance you should wear well-fitted, supportive shoes. Athletes have enough wear and tear on their knees, ankles and feet without going for a jog or jumping repetitively in improper footwear.

Develop Muscular Strength and Endurance

Muscular strength is the amount of force a muscle can exert or resist for a brief period of time. Research and practical experience tell us that if we stress a muscle or muscle group more than it is normally used to, it will eventually adapt and improve its function. Therefore, certain exercises are designed to increase strength so that we may perform our everyday activities with less exertion and less chance of injury. New research tells us that muscular strengthening exercises play a key part in preventing osteoporosis and preventing decreases in metabolism. If a muscle is stressed less than is usual, it will atrophy and lose strength. Broken limbs are good examples. The limb is immobilized for a length of time and when the cast is removed, the affected limb is usually smaller than the other. Professionals now agree that strength training should be an essential part of a complete athletic program.

> We all have dreams. But in order to make dreams come into reality, it takes an awful lot of determination, dedication, self-discipline, and effort.
>
> —Jesse Owens

Muscular endurance describes the ability of muscles to sustain repeated contractions or apply sustained force against a fixed object. If having muscular strength allows you to kick the ball once, then having muscular endurance allows you to kick it 50 times in one game. Activities such as skill drills, sit-ups, push-ups, raking leaves, shoveling snow, and pushing a lawn mower all require prolonged muscular exertion. Performing more repetitions with a lighter weight or resistance in your training will build muscular endurance. Safe and effective muscle training can be accomplished in practice, or on your own, with the help of a trainer.

Exercises utilizing weight training, calisthenics, and rubber bands will help to increase muscular strength and endurance. Usually three sets of 15 to 25 repetitions of each muscle exercise will accomplish this goal. Variety is important, so switching routines every couple of weeks will keep athletes from reaching a plateau in development.

Circuit training actually works well in a practice setting and it is easy to change the stations often to maintain variety.

Muscular Balance

Athletes can be at higher risk of injury when muscle strength in opposing muscle groups are unequal. Most athletes compensate for weakness by using one side more than the other—their "good" side—either by the position they play, or their throwing-dominant or kicking-dominant side, so that they end up overusing one side of a muscle group or one side of the body. Individuals often have sufficient strength in some muscle groups but are deficient in others. We use our quadriceps (thigh muscles) every time we kick, walk, run, climb stairs, so our hamstrings (back of the thigh) usually receive no significant exercise during everyday activities. The strong quadriceps and hip flexors pull with more force on the skeletal system, especially the hip, back, and knee. This kind of muscular imbalance is often the source of lower back pain and hip pain and make an athlete more prone to knee and other injuries. This also affects your posture, movement patterns, and can make you more vulnerable to injuries from other reasons. Thus, when using strength training you must concentrate on these weaker muscles to create balance.

A good rule to remember is: *Stretch the strong muscles and strengthen the weak ones!* If you have time, work on all of them.

Extra Strengthening for These Muscle Groups:

- Rectus abdominis, transverse abdominis, and internal and external obliques (abs)

- Erector spinae (lower back)

- Hamstrings (back of thigh)

- Abductor (outer thigh)

- Rhomboids (upper back)

- Deltoids (top of shoulders)

- Triceps (back of upper arm)

Include These Muscle Groups if You Have Time and Add Extra Stretching:

- Iliopsoas (hip flexors, front of hips)

- Quadriceps (front of thigh)

- Adductors (inner thigh)

- Gastrocnemius (calf muscles)

- Biceps (upper arm)

Functional Strength and Core Stabilization

Exercises, which help prepare you for real-life activities, require functional training. By re-creating the movement patterns you use in your daily activities you become stronger and more prepared for sports, work and recreation. Your mom or dad may only need enough fitness to mow the grass and bring in the groceries but an athlete needs a much higher level to perform successfully without injury. Focusing on coordination, balance, muscular control, and the speed of movements are some ways to work on functional fitness. Mimicking the actual movement when you exercise is a simple way to accomplish this. Try practicing the motions of swinging a tennis racquet but with weights or bands instead of the racquet. Athletes need a lot of abdominal core strength and oblique strength for most of their sport skills but not all of them have it. You can train for this by incorporating twisting and side crunches into a training program. It is also important to evaluate how much flexibility is necessary to excel and to prevent injury in your specific activities and to train with that goal in mind. For example, a football player or wrestler will be pushed or tackled into many extreme positions, which requires extraordinary flexibility.

Your core muscles include your abdominal muscles, your back muscles and smaller muscles involved in posture and support of the spine. Athletes should include exercises that focus on keeping the core muscles stable and strong as well as increasing strength during movement. Stability balls and standing exercises are great for improving core strength. Functional training should be used in conjunction with traditional strength training.

Flexibility

Flexibility is the range of motion possible around a joint. Stretching exercises are utilized to maintain or increase this range of movement, to help prevent muscle soreness, and to prevent long-term injuries. This is one of the most important and most neglected components of fitness for the athlete. Some athletes are naturally very flexible and others have to work much harder to obtain an adequate level. Studies have shown that stretching is most effective when performed at the end of the aerobic or muscular workout, when the muscles are warm all the way to the core. For most sports, it is necessary to stretch gently in the beginning of practice, or before the game after the circulatory warm-up, but the more intense stretching should be at the end.

Since flexibility is specific to every joint, it is incorrect to refer to flexibility in a general sense, e.g. "Joe has good flexibility." Each joint must be evaluated separately. Another common misconception is to assume that to have good flexibility, a person must have an excessive amount. There are some athletes, who are so flexible that it is difficult to control movement or they are very injury- prone. Athletes often place their bodies in positions that stretch muscles and connective tissue beyond the point deemed necessary for normal function. They do this for the sake of competition or aesthetics, which requires special coaching and conditioning to avoid injuries. A well-trained coach or personal trainer will be able to gradually improve and maintain your flexibility level for all joints.

Body Composition

Your body weight includes the weight of all your muscles, bones, organs, body fluids, and body fat. If the fat is removed, all that remains is your lean body mass. Too much adipose tissue (fat) has been associated with many health risks including heart disease, diabetes, hypertension, arthritis, gall bladder disease, cirrhosis of the liver, hernia, intestinal problems, and sleep disorders. Aerobic, strength, and endurance programs will increase the lean body mass and decrease body fat.

Your percentage of body fat is a much better indicator of your fitness than your weight. Many athletes would be considered overweight according to typical weight charts. However, if we measured their percentage of body fat, it would probably be low or within normal ranges. There are also many thin, sedentary people who weigh very little but have a high percentage of body fat. It would be dangerous for these individuals to lose weight—they must exercise to increase their lean muscle mass. Do not become discouraged if you weigh more than your friends who do not play sports. Chances are that wonderful muscle of yours just makes you weigh a little more on the scales.

Long-term regular exercise usually decreases body fat but it does not always have an immediate effect on body weight. This is because you are gaining muscle mass as you lose the fat. If you are trying to lose excess weight, do not become discouraged if your weight does not change immediately. Remember that your body composition is improving. If you can imagine the fat cells in your body just hanging out, not needing much (fuel, oxygen, etc.), not doing much—just there. Now picture your muscle cells—constantly using energy, needing huge deliveries of oxygen, and staying very busy. Because lean (muscle) tissue is more metabolically active than fat, you will burn more calories all of the time, even when you are sitting around or sleeping. Exercise also increases your ability to mobilize and oxidize fat. This enhances weight loss efforts, conserving lean body mass and preventing the regaining of lost body fat. If you are working out a lot and still feel like you need to decrease fat and increase muscle, you might need to focus on the food you are eating. The right exercise and optimal diet are both necessary to achieve optimal body composition.

Body fat varies widely even between fit individuals. We do know that the average person in the United States tends to be overly fat. Women are considered to be obese at a body fat of 32% or higher, men at 25% or higher. Women are considered fit at 21 to 24% body-fat, and men at 14 to 17% although young athletes tend to be much lower. Females who drop below 10 to 13% may cease menstruating. This decreased estrogen level promotes calcium loss from the bones, increasing the risk of fractures and osteoporosis. This is a common problem for those with eating disorders, long distance runners, and other extreme endurance athletes. As a female athlete, if you stop menstruating for more than three months, make sure you consult your doctor. It could be that you are training too hard and/or not eating enough calories.

Understanding the components of fitness helps you know how to train to improve the ones you need to improve for your sport.

3. Why Warm Up?

A thletes often make the mistake of equating the words "warm-up" and "stretching." They are not the same and they comprise two separate parts of your pre-training or game routine. Many athletes start practice with a few toe-touches or side-bends. Although stretching exercises should be included before vigorous activity or your game, the most important goal is to increase the body temperature and to prepare the muscles, connective tissue, and circulatory system to safely accommodate more intense movement. Stretching cold can be more harmful than not stretching at all. A proper warm-up improves performance, allows you to focus, and reduces the chance of injury and muscle soreness.

The warm-up is divided into three parts:

The Circulatory or Thermal Warm-up

The circulatory warm-up should be designed to raise your core temperature and the local temperature of muscles, ligaments, and tendons, to increase blood flow to the working muscles and to increase your rate of breathing. It involves continuous, rhythmic, full-body movement like walking, marching, light jogging, prancing, or hopping. Improved blood flow will bring oxygen and nutrients to your cells and help to remove waste products. Your energy systems are activated to provide more fuel for your muscles and your heart rate starts to increase to accommodate the upcoming strenuous movement. The higher body temperature allows nervous impulses to travel faster which maximizes coordination. In your muscle, the mechanical efficiency of contraction is enhanced so your muscle contractions can be quicker and more forceful.

This warm-up might only last 5 or 10 minutes on a warm day or could take 10 to 15 minutes in a cold environment. Remember that no stretching should be included during this segment. The circulatory warm-up should continue until a light perspiration is present. At this point you should not feel tired or out of breath. Your heart rate and breathing are slightly elevated, your muscles are warmer, and you are ready to begin range of motion warm-ups. Advanced athletes need a longer warm-up than beginners. The more in shape you are and the harder you train, the longer it takes to achieve the same effects from your warm-up.

The Range of Motion Warm-up

The movement in this section is designed to lubricate your joints and prepare them for more intense activity. You should mimic patterns and paths that your body will soon be required to perform. Bend and straighten knees and elbows. Roll your ankles, wrists, shoulders, and torso. Move your body front to back, side to side, and up and down. If your coach does not include this type of warm-up, you may need to arrive early do this on your own.

The Stretching Warm-up

Now you are warm, your muscles are more elastic and your tendons, ligaments, and other connective tissues are ready to lengthen and stretch. Warm tissues stretch more easily, providing more permanent results and less risk of injury. Equal stretching of each joint will improve your posture and body symmetry, increase range of motion, delay the onset of muscle fatigue, and minimize soreness. Never violently force a stretch. Notice signs that you may be overextending your limits. There is a difference between the discomfort of stretching and actual pain. Some athletes are naturally very flexible and others have to spend much time on this part of their training. If you are trying to improve your flexibility, you might need to warm-up and spend time stretching on your own.

Types of Stretching

Ballistic stretching consists of quick, repetitive, bouncing type movements. The momentum can result in damage to muscle and connective tissue and may be responsible for increased muscle soreness. This is not the best method for beginning athletes or for recovery from injuries, but in special circumstances it may help advanced athletes prepare for challenging and vigorous competition. Sports like football, gymnastics, and wrestling probably need some ballistic stretching to make sure you are prepared for the requirements and aggressive movements of your sport.

Static Stretching involves gradually going into a position of stretch until tension is felt. The position is then held for 10 to 30 seconds or even longer. Since static stretching is more controlled, there is less chance of exceeding the limits of the tissue thereby creating injury. Research shows that after six seconds, a stretch reflex kicks in and allows the muscle to relax. This is why after you hold for a while, you can then stretch a little farther.

Dynamic stretching involves moving slowly and with control through a range of motion. You must have completed a thermal warm-up for this to be safe. Some dynamic stretching is recommended in all sports.

Contract and Relax methods involve contraction of muscles or muscle groups for 5 to 10 seconds followed by relaxing and stretching with extra pressure. Traditionally, this procedure has been utilized by physical therapists but it can be used very successfully with athletes. Use this method with caution, as some of the positions require a partner, which may increase the risk of overstretching and consequent injury. A great way to learn new techniques is to hire a personal trainer who can help you design a specific stretching program for your flexibility level and specific goals.

Active Isolated Flexibility was developed by Jim (exercise physiologist) and Phil (sports therapist) Wharton and is performed with a rope. It involves contracting a muscle to relax the targeted muscle in preparation of its stretch. This is a very effective technique but requires proper instruction or use of a video training program.

The Final Stretch

Many coaches and athletes forget, or run out of time for stretching at the end of practice or the game. Research shows that this is the best time to stretch and gain increased range of motion. The muscles are warm all the way to the core, and it is safer to push the limits of your flexibility.

THE FINAL SCORE

HOME 7   VISITORS 3

Warming up and stretching are not the same thing. You must warm-up to increase your body temperature and blood flow, to increase metabolism, improve coordination, and to prevent muscle injury. Stretch only after you are warm and sweating slightly. Remember to stretch at the very end of practice for the best results.

4. Advanced Training Techniques for the Serious Athlete

Know the Requirements of Your Sport

Before any athlete begins training intensely, it is important that they understand which components of fitness are necessary for success in their particular sport, playing position, and level of competition.

Here is a checklist:

Type of sport_____

Position(s) played _____

Level of competition

- ❏ Middle school

- ❏ Travel team/club sports

- ❏ High school

- ❏ Collegiate

❏ Olympic level

❏ Professional level

Physical Requirements:

Check all that apply or you can rank them:

❏ Cardiovascular endurance (keep moving for more than two minutes continuously)

❏ Muscular strength (move or resist heavy objects or other athletes)

❏ Muscular endurance (strong, fast movements continually without a break)

❏ Flexibility (large range of movement required)

❏ Agility (quick changes of direction or movement)

❏ Explosive power (jumping and strong, fast movements)

❏ Speed (anaerobic endurance)

❏ Technical skills and accuracy (success depends on accurate execution of technique)

Other Requirements:

❏ Mental focus (ability to concentrate for long periods)

❏ Confidence (required to be a leader and role model, take initiative for scoring)

❏ Commitment (long training sessions, grueling game and travel schedule)

❏ Mental toughness (have to endure significant fatigue or discomfort)

❏ Decision making (have to decide quickly where to move, pass, or hit)

❏ Knowledge of strategy

❏ Ability to work as a team member

❏ Control of your emotions (physical contact with other players, decisions of officials, etc.)

Requirements for All Successful Athletes

❏ Proper nutrition

❏ Management of oxidative stress (fruit and vegetable consumption)

❏ Hydration

❏ Adequate rest and sleep

❏ Stress management skills

List your strengths as a high-achieving athlete

List attributes you wish to improve with additional training

_____

List the time(s) of the year you need to hit peak performance for your sport

_____

Your coach or personal trainer will help design your training program so you will be at the top of your training program at the right time for competition. This is called "peaking." Many athletes need to peak several times per year or be at their best for an entire season. Ask for help in customizing your training program to assure you will achieve your goals.

Muscle Confusion and Plateaus

Changing your workout routine often and maintaining a variety of training techniques will help you avoid a plateau in your improvement. Once the body becomes used to a routine it is harder to see increases in strength and endurance. Muscle confusion is a technique to counteract this lack of improvement that occurs when muscles adapt to a specific training program. Vary the weight, sets, reps, rest and exercise angles used during each workout. You can alter your workout every couple of weeks or every workout depending on the sport and your goals.

> Athletes will find support and encouragement from parents, coaches and teammates alike. But understand this, there is no substitute for hard work, great nutrition and plenty of sleep.
>
> —Adam Ciarla, Certified Personal Trainer,
> Owner of Ciarla Fitness, Inc.

Muscular Strength and Endurance

Strength is the force you can apply by using your muscles. Muscular endurance is usually measured by counting the number of times you can perform a movement before fatigue sets in. Both fitness goals can usually be accomplished by resistance training which may include: calisthenics using your own body weight (push-ups), weigh training with machines, free weights, or resistance bands.

The following prescription should be used to increase overall strength, endurance and muscle balance: focus more on strength, increase the weight and decrease the repetitions; and focus more on endurance, decrease the weight, and increase the repetitions. The American College of Sports Medicine recommends at least two non-consecutive days per week, although three days would allow faster progress. Some athletes do weight training every day but they alternate muscle groups. An example would be: on Mon/Wed/Fri —work on arms, chest, and back, and them on Tue/Thur/Sat— work on legs and abs. These suggestions depend on your level of achievement, your goals, and the time available.

> Being successful is not an accident. It is the result of preparation, hard work, and sacrifice. Results are like an investment, the more you put into it, the better the results.
>
> —Jim Cerbie, Varsity Baseball Coach, Providence Day School

General Guidelines:

Sets: perform 1 to 3 sets with weights or bands. Three sets are optimal especially during the pre-season. You can maintain your strength gains with one set once the season starts.

Repetitions: begin at 8 repetitions, and work up to 12. This gives you the best mix of strength and endurance. When 12 are easy, increase the weight slightly and go back to 8 repetitions. This way you will continue to increase strength and endurance.

Weight or Resistance: choose a weight so that you feel the fatigue on the last 3 to 4 repetitions. Young athletes under 14 should stick with fairly light weights and do more repetitions.

Vary Your Workout: every few weeks or months, change your workout slightly so you will continue to improve. You can change the type of exercise, the number of repetitions, the speed of the contraction, etc.

> Keep your emotions under control. If I came to the game in the sixth inning not knowing the score, I should not be able to tell whether you're winning or losing by your body language.
>
> —Jim Cerbie, Varsity Baseball Coach, Providence Day School

Safety Tips for Strength Training:

• Never perform muscle work without completing a circulatory warm-up. Ten minutes of light jogging or fast walking will work.

• Lift weights only with an adult or a qualified spotter present.

• Utilize proper form and body position. If any position or exercise causes discomfort it should be discontinued immediately. The back and the knee are most vulnerable to injury, so avoid locking the knee and never hyperextend (excessive arch) the lower back while lifting weights.

- Slower is better for beginners. Once you have a base of strength and general fitness you can learn to train more for power. Many high-level athletes use too much momentum when weight training. Try doing super-slow reps for some of your workouts. New studies show significant increases in strength with this method.

- When performing standing exercises, bend your knees and keep the natural arch in your back. This is called the "neutral pelvic position" and keeps your spine in the best position to support weight and movement.

Interval training

Interval training is a powerful technique for athletes and for people who just want to improve their fitness and promote weight loss. Many sports require bursts of energy for 1 to 4 minutes followed by complete rest or lighter activity, and then the burst is repeated. Interval training is simply alternating the periods of intense activity with intervals of lighter activity during your practices or training sessions. During intense exercise, muscles produce lactic acid, a waste product. Too much lactic acid can make exercise painful and exhausting. By alternating bursts of intense exercise with easier intervals, you'll help reduce the buildup of lactic acid in your muscles. Your body will become more efficient at moving the lactic acid out between bouts of activity.

It you want to do interval training on your own, start with walking. If you're in good shape, you might incorporate short bursts of jogging into your regular brisk walks. If you're less fit, you might alternate leisurely walking with periods of faster walking. For example, if you're walking outdoors, you could walk faster between certain mailboxes, trees or other landmarks. There is no set length or intensity for the intervals; it is up to your coach, your trainer, or up to you. The only rule is that you have to complete a circulatory warm-up before you begin.

Benefits of Interval Training:

- You'll burn more calories. The more vigorously you exercise, the more calories you'll burn — even if you increase intensity for just a few minutes at a time.

- You'll improve your aerobic capacity. As your cardiovascular fitness improves, you'll be able to exercise longer or with more intensity.

- It adds variety and reduces boredom. Turning up your intensity in short intervals can add variety to your exercise routine.

- You don't need special equipment. You can simply modify your current routine.

Safety Precautions for Interval Training:

Even trained athletes should start slowly when utilizing a new exercise plan. If you rush into a strenuous workout before your body is ready, you may injure your muscles, tendons or bones. Instead, start slowly. Try just one or two higher intensity intervals during each workout at first. If you think you're overdoing it, slow down. As your stamina improves, challenge yourself to vary the pace. You may be surprised by the results.

Circuit Training

Circuit training is designed to combine cardiovascular training with strength, endurance, power and agility moves. You can do this on your own, with a trainer, or with your coach and the rest of your team. Set up a series of exercises in a circle. I usually use 6 to 12 stations depending on how many athletes are going to participate and my goal for training them that day. Alternate the aerobic stations with strength and other moves. You can use timed stations or a set number of repetitions. Start each player at a different station. One benefit to this method is that you can work every muscle group and keep your heart rate up during the entire workout. You can make your circuits very specific to your goals and your sport.

Sample Circuit for Basketball Players—do each station continuously for one minute.

- **Station One:** Jump rope

- **Station Two:** Jump squats

- **Station Three:** Walking lunges with shoulder press (weighted ball)

- **Station Four:** Push-ups (on knees for beginners) or bench press

- **Station Five:** High knee agility drill through cones

- **Station Six:** Sideways gallop (30 seconds on each side/can be done on a treadmill with incline)

- **Station Seven:** Abdominal crunches

- **Station Eight**: Up-Up Down-Down footwork drill, on and off a step. For 30 seconds-lead with right foot, then for 30 seconds-lead with left foot

- **Station Nine**: Seated row

- **Station Ten**: Jump squats (toes turned out)

- **Station Eleven:** Power chest pass to coach or trainer with weighted ball

- **Station Twelve:** Triceps dips on weight machine or a bench

Start over and repeat for a total of three circuits.

Plyometrics: Training for Explosive Power (Speed/ Strength/Agility)

Plyometrics is a method of training for and developing explosive power. Sometimes it is called "speed-strength" training. This is because you are trying to reach your maximum strength in an intense movement and in the shortest period of time. Almost all athletes can benefit, but especially sprinters, jumpers, hurdlers, throwers, and weight lifters. The most common sports that utilize plyometrics are football, wrestling, basketball, skiing, soccer, gymnastics, dancing, tennis, cycling and volleyball. We know that the concept of progressive overload (working muscles harder than they are normally accustomed to working) builds strength, endurance, and power. By performing exercises and movements that emphasize strength, speed, and agility and taking them to the point of overload, an athlete should see an improvement in specific skills like leaping, jumping, and lifting. If you choose to add plyometrics to your workouts, make sure that your coach is trained to teach you, or enlist a certified personal trainer to help you develop a program.

Safety is very important because you will be working at a very high intensity. Techniques for jumping, landing, foot placement, and posture are crucial for success. The principle of specificity is very important in plyometrics. Specificity means concentrating on a particular or specific individual or group of muscles, or areas of improvement.

Training that mimics the same angles and contractions that you will be using in your performance will also improve neuromuscular skills.

You will experience more muscle soreness with this intense kind of training. The breakdown of muscle tissue and recovery is part of the process of increasing power. So a day of rest between workouts is usually required. Research has shown that young athletes will see improvement with 2 to 3 training sessions per week.

Other Specific Training Techniques for Athletes

Active-Isolated Strength and Flexibility Programs

These training systems are designed to pinpoint, isolate and strengthen individual muscles. Developed by Jim (exercise physiologist) and Phil (sports therapist) Wharton, these methods reduce your workload by removing tightness, so that you can swing your limbs more freely. These stretches transport oxygen to sore muscles and quickly remove toxins from muscles, so recovery is faster for athletes of all levels. Most of the exercises are practiced with a rope with each exercise designed to work or stretch a specific muscle group. The best way to learn these techniques is to attend a class or learn from a video (see Recommended Resources).

Pilates

Pilates or physical mind method, is a series of non-impact exercises designed by Joseph Pilates to develop strength, flexibility, balance, and inner awareness. This method strengthens and lengthens muscles without causing bulk which is perfect for athletes who need to maintain flexibility, which is almost all of them. Posture, core strength, balance, and circulation will all be improved. The best way to incorporate Pilates into your training is to have a certified instructor visit your team, take a class from a certified instructor, or learn from a video.

Rest restores. The best athletes are the ones who discipline themselves all the way around: fitness, diet and rest. There is nothing worse to watch than a beautiful athlete too tired to deliver. My nephew, a Division One scholarship swimmer, started swimming competitively and daily in the 8th grade. He made his best times after a six-month injury-related rest.

—Mary Yorke Oates, High school and collegiate athlete, basketball and field hockey coach, former US Olympic Development Coach

Yoga

The term *yoga* comes from a Sanskrit word which means yoke or union. Yoga postures are used to tone, strengthen and align the body. These postures are performed to make the spine supple and healthy and to promote blood flow to all the organs, glands, and tissues, keeping all the bodily systems healthy. Mentally, yoga uses breathing techniques and meditation to quiet and discipline the mind. Athletes benefit from yoga in many ways. It is a great time to focus on the mind-body connection and to develop better health and fitness in general. A qualified instructor is crucial to making sure your yoga postures are performed with proper technique. Yoga is also great when an athlete is rehabilitating an injury.

Tapering: The Power of Rest

Many athletes train year round and have several times during the year when they need to hit a "peak performance." Tapering is a training technique designed to reverse the fatigue that occurs during heavy training, without losing

any training benefits that you have worked so hard to achieve. It is the final phase of training prior to important competitions and it involves a reduction in training load, by lowering training intensity, frequency and duration.

The word "peaking" is also used in conjunction with the concept of tapering. The period of time required for an optimal taper will vary depending on the athlete, the type of sport, and the time available between competitions or games. A taper period that is too long in duration or reduces training volume too rapidly may not provide sufficient training stimulus to prevent losing what you have gained. A taper period that is too short or one that fails to reduce training volume sufficiently will not allow enough time for full physiological and mental recovery.

Here are some benefits of an effective taper:

- More glycogen in the leg muscles (this also depends on proper dietary intake)

- Increased density of red blood cells

- Increased blood plasma

- Increased enzyme activity in the leg muscles

- Increased size of muscle fibers (increased strength and power)

- Increased maximal oxygen uptake (better aerobic ability)

- Improvement in the neural system (coordination, reaction time, and agility)

Taper periods range from 4 to 28 days. Shorter tapers are usually necessary when competitions and games are within weeks or days of each other. Research has shown that tapering produces improvements in performance of 1% to 22%.

A less technical approach to tapering would be to simply pay attention to your sleep habits and your ability to rest between training sessions, practices, and games. When things get too busy and intense, your body will respond with more sickness and signs of over-training. One of the best skills to develop as an athlete is the ability to listen to your body.

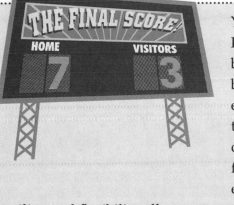

You are an athlete. In order for your body to be at its best for competitive events, it must first be trained to utilize all of the components of fitness. Power, speed, endurance, strength, agility, and flexibility all come together to allow you to maximize your skills in practice or the game.

Pre-season training will prepare you physically
so you can concentrate on mastering the skills
you need to beat your competition.

— Will B., age 14

Football, Basketball, Lacrosse player

5. Basic Injury Prevention & Treatment

A thletes occasionally have to deal with chronic and acute injuries. They usually have a high pain tolerance and they sometimes ignore small injuries until they become more bothersome with painful symptoms. Coaches should spend a great deal of time on muscle balance, flexibility, posture, and alignment, because excessive tension on joints is the most common cause of chronic injuries. Learning to listen carefully to what your body is telling you is a crucial skill for all athletes. Look for patterns in how your body feels. You might want to keep a journal of which movements cause discomfort or pain. Are you favoring one side over the other? This will help a sports medicine professional diagnose more accurately. Prevention is best, but when injuries do occur you have to adjust your practice schedule and recognize and treat the problem.

Those who think they have no time for healthy eating will sooner or later have to find time for illness.

Edward Stanley (1826 1893) from *The Conduct of Life*

Daily Checklist for Athlete Injury Prevention, Safety, and Health

- Am I hydrated?

- Have I eaten a small meal recently to provide energy for this activity?

- Have I checked the playing surface for obstacles, sharp objects or stray equipment?

- Do I have the proper shoes for this activity?

- Have I performed a circulatory warm-up to prepare my joints?

- Am I focused and ready to concentrate?

The PRICE Treatment for Sports Injuries

The most important and urgent aspect of this sports injury treatment is the cold element. Several things happen when ice is applied to injured tissue. First, the blood vessels constrict, decreasing blood flow to the area. This reduces bleeding and, therefore, swelling. Cold also acts as an anesthetic, controlling pain and relieving muscle spasms. Ice slows down metabolism around the injury, slowing the release of histamine that increases inflammation and swelling. You can use ice packs, ice baths, or ice massages. Apply as quickly as possible. The formula involves:

PROTECTION: Protect the area from additional injury (maybe a splint or crutches).

REST: Stop immediately when you feel pain.

ICE: Apply ice for 15 minutes several times per day with at least 20 minutes off between applications. Use ice bags, cold packs or even a bag of frozen peas, wrapped in a thin towel, to provide cold to the injured area. Cold can provide short-term pain relief. It also limits swelling by reducing blood flow to the injured area. Limit the ice to 15 minutes. Longer exposure can damage your skin.

COMPRESSION: Firmly wrap the injured area (not too tightly) with elastic (ACE®) or compression bandages. Bandages should reach from the largest area below the injury up to the largest area above the injury. If it starts throbbing, rewrap a little more loosely. Compression limits swelling, which slows down healing, and compression can reduce pain.

ELEVATION: Raise the affected area level with, or slightly above, the heart to encourage blood flow to and from the injury.

Heat should never be applied too soon or it will increase swelling and bleeding into tissues. Within at least 72 hours after the injury, use heat (warm, not hot) to increase blood flow to the area. Oxygen delivery is then increased and waste products are removed. Apply 2 to 3 times a day for 20 to 30 minutes at a time. After two or three days, you can alternate cold with heat (contrast bath)—hot for 1 to 2 minutes (96 to 98 degrees) and then cold (55 to 64 degrees) for 1 to 2 minutes. Repeat several times and finish with cold for five minutes. In all cases, if pain becomes worse or persists for a prolonged period, seek medical attention immediately. Gentle massage and stretching exercises can be added after the acute phase of injury has passed. Proceed slowly upon resuming your activity.

Common Injuries Associated with Exercise

Muscle Soreness (Delayed Onset Muscle Soreness)

When muscles break down and repair themselves, the result is a stronger muscle; therefore mild muscle soreness may be a good sign. Muscle soreness usually occurs when you begin a new exercise regimen, perform eccentric contractions (lengthening the muscle), or change your normal training routine. Attending a camp or practice with a guest coach, or embarking on a new strength training routine will challenge your body in different ways and cause soreness. Microscopic tears in the muscle or connective tissue may require several days of rest for tissue repair and rebuilding. Severe soreness is unnecessary.

The key is prevention. Proceed slowly. Start with a smaller number of repetitions and lower intensity, and make sure you warm-up and cool-down properly. Avoid ballistic movements and stretches. If you do become sore, it will usually last 24 to 48 hours regardless of what you do to treat it. Sometimes repeating mild exercise the following day and then performing slow, static stretches will relieve some of the discomfort. Massage and warm baths may also help.

Foot Injuries

The equipment that you use most in athletics is attached to each of your legs. Taking care of your feet is one of the most commonly overlooked aspects of sports training. Common complaints that affect athletes include rubbing shoes, tired, aching feet and foot pain. Start with professional fitting of your shoes. Other common foot problems are blisters, corns and calluses, athlete's foot, heel pain, over-pronation, and sesamoiditis. Blisters should not be broken—let them dry out. Try cutting moleskin into a donut shape to protect the blister. See the resource Web site for sites that will help you find help in treating foot problems.

Shin Splints

Inflammation or pain occurring where the muscles and tendons attach to bones can cause pain in the front portion of the lower leg. This can result from running barefoot, poorly fitted shoes, an improper running surface, or from a program which is too intense. An imbalance between the gastrocnemius (calf muscle) and the tibialis anterior (shin muscle) may also contribute to shin problems. Other causes of shin splints include a lowered arch (flat feet), decreased flexibility in the Achilles tendon, irritated membranes, tearing of muscle where it attaches to bone, a hairline or stress fracture of the bone, or other factors. The best treatment is the PRICE treatment, however, stopping the aggravating activity and switching to a low impact activity for a while may allow time for healing while maintaining fitness. See a medical doctor to rule out fractures.

Helpful Hint: You may need supportive inserts for your shoes. This gives the foot and leg more cushioning and arch support.

Knee Problems

Pain in the knee can be very difficult to diagnose. Many times it is the result of overuse, poorly fitted shoes, improper surfaces, or biomechanical problems. Using a proper progression, avoiding uneven surfaces, making sure your muscles are balanced, and not allowing injuries to become chronic will help prevent serious knee problems. Always see a physician and physical therapist if pain persists.

Ankle Problems

Ankle sprains are the most common ankle injury. Prevention includes strengthening exercises, adequate warm-up, proper footwear and ankle bracing. Activities that require quick changes of direction or exercises performed on an uneven surface may increase the chance of sprains. If an ankle injury should occur, the ankle should be iced immediately and medical treatment should be sought.

Helpful Hint: Check your playing field or surface for uneven spots, holes, or debris, which can cause your ankle to turn over.

Achilles Tendonitis

Achilles tendonitis, which is an inflammation of the sheath around the Achilles tendon, can cause severe pain and is a frequent complaint of athletes and distance runners. Usually, improper shoes and lack of flexibility are the culprits, and stretching, or ice and rest, are the treatment.

Side Stitch

This is a sharp pain in the side beneath the ribs. Possible causes for this pain include: an oxygen deficiency, gas pains, and spasms of the diaphragm or an improper warm-up. Often it will disappear if you lower the intensity of your activity, take slow, deep breaths, or bend toward the stitch and press gently on the painful area. Make sure you are not eating too large a meal or a meal too high in fat or sugar before you exercise, as this will cause cramping.

Heat Injuries

In extremely hot temperatures or high humidity you need to be very careful to avoid heat cramps, heat exhaustion, and heat stroke. Heat cramps are the mildest heat-stress problem. Symptoms include muscle twitches and cramping in the arms, legs, and abdomen. Heat exhaustion is more serious. Symptoms include headache, dizziness, severe fatigue, nausea, low urinary output, and weak and rapid pulse. If you experience any of these symptoms, you should cool off and drink fluids containing potassium. Heat stroke causes hot, dry, flushed skin, incoherent behavior, an inability to perspire, and seizures. If not treated, heat stroke can be fatal so medical attention is required immediately. To reduce the risk of heat injuries drink 8 to 10 eight-ounce glasses of water per day and avoid extreme activity in the heat of the day or in an overly hot environment.

Training too frequently, too intensely, or for long durations may predispose you to injuries. Never "work through the pain." Learn your body's patterns and imbalances and seek help to correct them. Spend extra time on strength and flexibility. Seek the appropriate treatment from a qualified sports medicine professional or physical therapist.

PMA—Positive Mental Attitude goes a long way.

When you get into the batter's box, your mindset
should be, 'How hard am I going to hit this
pitch,' and not 'Am I going to hit this pitch.'

Every time the pitcher throws a pitch,
expect it to be a good one to hit.

Swing hard just in case you hit it!

—Jim Cerbie, Varsity Baseball Coach, Providence Day School

6. Focus and Mental Preparation for Athletics

—with Charee Boulter, PhD, Psychologist

Performance Anxiety

Most athletes fear they will experience performance anxiety. You might have an image of yourself before a game or competition with butterflies in your stomach, fearing you will fail. Your image might include the spectators laughing or your coach being angry with you. Whatever your mental picture of a failed performance may be, your ability to imagine it helps you to understand why athletes sometimes experience performance anxiety.

It is important to know that even the best athletes experience anxiety. How an athlete manages his or her anxiety is one of the keys to success. At the elite level, all of the athletes are highly skilled and talented. They have spent years training and competing. When you see them in action, the athletes who appear to be one with their sport, moving effortlessly, are well prepared mentally.

Benefits of mental preparation

Stress or anxiety is a part of life. Learning to manage anxiety as an athlete will help you improve your physical abilities and will help you manage stress in other aspects of your life. Great success occurs when an athlete believes in the *possibility*, in addition to having dedication, practice and talent.

Here is a list of some of the positive benefits of mental preparation:

- Increased self confidence
- Improved focus during practice and in competition
- Decreased fear and anxiety
- Increased enjoyment of your sport
- Enhanced performance
- Improved ability to manage stress

Aspects of mental preparation

Create a positive frame of mind

Our way of thinking, positively or negatively, impacts the outcome of our efforts. When you maintain a positive focus you increase the likelihood of success. Consider the effect of steering while riding a bicycle. You steer in the direction that you want to go. Likewise, positive thinking is "steering" your mind and body in the direction you want to take your sport.

The first step in creating a positive approach is to be aware of your thoughts.

• Notice when you have positive and negative thoughts.

• Notice how you feel when you have positive thoughts.

• Notice how you feel when you have negative thoughts.

Many athletes feel energized and relaxed when they have positive thoughts. Negative thoughts often lead to feeling nervous, stressed, tired, or unmotivated.

The greater the conflict, the more rewarding the outcome.

—James C., High School Athlete, Grade 11

Be aware that both negative and positive thoughts are normal parts of life. The goal of creating a positive mindset is not to remove all negative thoughts or judgments. Some of our negative thoughts are important information that helps us. For example, when preparing a snack, if you notice the food you are about to eat has a strange smell, your thought is, "This food is rotten!" This negative judgment is important and will help you avoid becoming ill. However, negative thoughts can hurt your performance. If you are struggling and find yourself thinking, "I will never get this. I am so uncoordinated," then your mindset is interfering with your ability to learn the skill.

- Recognize your thoughts are just thoughts—not predictions of reality.

- Reframe your negative thoughts that interfere with your performance into positive thoughts or challenges.

An example: "I just can't jump high enough." When you recognize this is just a thought, you can reframe it and create a positive challenge. "I am aware that I am struggling. I wonder what I can do differently. Maybe this is an opportunity to work with my coach to enhance my power and strength."

By changing how you think about a situation you direct your attention toward your goal. You want to steer your mind's eye (thoughts) in the direction that you ultimately want to go.

This year I was one of the younger and less experienced players on my lacrosse team. One day I was frustrated because the game was close and I never was put in to play. My dad brought me home and we watched the movie 'Rudy' together. Now I just work really hard at practice and focus on my skills and teamwork so I'll be ready when I do get a chance to play. I highly recommend this movie to all athletes.

—Will B., Football, Basketball, Lacrosse Player, Age 14

Set goals:

Think about what you would ideally like to be doing as an athlete in 5 to 10 years. Go ahead and dream big. Remember, believing in the possibility is a key ingredient to your success. Write your goal down. Keep this someplace where you can see it. Sometimes we get so busy with daily life that we lose sight of our dreams and settle for less. Even if you don't achieve your dream goal, you will achieve at higher levels by setting your sights high. If your goal is only one or two steps above your current level you will limit your possibilities.

Look at your 5- to 10-year goal. What do you think is involved in achieving it? Talk to your coach to find out what you need to do. Talk to your parents to see if they can support you in achieving this goal. Make a list of what you need to do and set smaller, intermediate goals.

An example: I want to play my sport in college.

Coach's feedback:

• Need to train 3 to 4 hours daily in season

• Need to maintain fitness off-season

• Need to attend summer camp

Parents' feedback:

- Supportive of increased daily practice, if I can still maintain my academic progress and household responsibilities

- Financially, they can help support summer camp if I raise some of the money

- They offer their support and suggest that I maintain both athletic and academic goals.

- They want me to go to college for an education.

Now focus on today and the next six months. It is important to have goals to guide you today. You should have a few goals specific to your sport. It is also important to include aspects of your life that are related, such as getting enough sleep, eating right, and finding a way to balance time with school, family, friends and sports.

Examples:

- Stay after team practice for extra strength and flexibility training three times per week

- Stop by school office next week and schedule an appointment within the next two weeks

- Talk to school counselor for ideas about time management so I can maintain my grades while training more

• Develop a financial plan with my parents and come up with ways to raise money to attend summer camp

• Share my goals and plans with friends that I plan to increase practice time

• Schedule quality time with friends so we keep the friendships active, while seeing less of each other

Positive affirmations:

Positive affirmations help you maintain your focus in the moment. They are short statements you repeat to yourself. Affirmations can help you manage anxiety and steer your mind in the direction you want to go. Affirmations are stated positively, focusing on what you want to achieve. Affirmations are about who you are becoming. They help you build confidence in your possibilities and in your current abilities.

Examples:

• I am good at changing direction.

• My legs are strong—my jumps are high.

• My serve is strong and powerful.

• I am good at seeing my teammates who are open.

• I am a strong defender.

• My endurance is good even at the end of the game.

- My teammates look to me as a leader.

- I am confident in my ability to score.

- I know all of the plays and have committed them to memory.

Focus on goals while rehearsing:

Prior to practice, review your short-term goals and affirmations. Make an effort to train as if you were in competition. Practice with the confidence and focus of a professional athlete. It is important to be mentally focused and physically disciplined. The more often you train as if you are competing, the easier it is to make the transition to the playing field. You want to practice with intentions of greatness to train your body to perform during competition.

Concentration

Some days it can be difficult to focus on your sport. You may have an important test to study for or maybe you had a disagreement with a friend. When you find that your mind is wandering during practice, try to refocus. This may be challenging. Here are some strategies that can help:

- Remind yourself that now is time for your sport—you can study when you leave practice

- Make time to deal with the stressor—time to study, time to talk to your friend

- Focus on your coach's voice when your mind wanders

- Focus on your breathing when your mind wanders

The goal is to bring your attention back to your body and your sport. If you are training and thinking about other aspects of your life, you are not fully focused. In this state you are more likely to get injured. It is important that you deal with the issue creating the distraction. If you use your sport as a place to escape, the issue will not resolve itself.

Visual imagery

Using your imagination to create a perfect performance allows you the opportunity to rehearse mentally. Recall the beginning of the chapter when you imagined how it would feel to fail or have performance anxiety. If you can imagine a mistake and feel the related embarrassment and anxiety, then you can also imagine a perfect performance. Using visual imagery is similar to using positive thinking. It is important to visualize your desired performance. Visual imagery is an important component of mental preparation. When you imagine your performance, your muscles are activated, therefore, by imagining your peak performance you are priming your muscles to repeat the performance.

Many athletes find it is easier to learn how to practice visualization after experiencing Guided Visualization. Ask your coach if she/he knows somebody who can teach you.

You can begin on your own by following these steps to achieve a relaxed state:

• Find a quiet place without distractions

• Do some deep breathing to help your body relax

• Focus your mind on the sensations of your body as you breath in and out

• Notice any muscle tension and try to relax as you exhale

After relaxing for a few minutes begin visualizing your peak or desired performance. You may view yourself, as if you were watching a video. Imagine the movements flowing easily, being one with your sport. You may notice that sometimes as you visualize, you truly feel your sport and experience it from within, rather than as a video. Either form of visualizing can be effective.

Some athletes find that it takes a while to visualize a complete performance. Begin with only as much as you can visualize. You might work on visualizing a challenging aspect of your sport. You might visualize yourself feeling confident and managing your anxiety prior to or during a competition. Use your imagination to help build your confidence in yourself and your athletic abilities.

Anxiety Management

Remember that anxiety is not necessarily good or bad. It is what you do with the experience of anxiety and the intensity of the anxiety that determines how it will affect you. The optimal level of anxiety is often described as excitement or anticipation. At this level, anxiety is motivating. Too much anxiety is experienced as stress, intimidation or fear. You can change your response to heightened anxiety through physical, mental or emotional channels. Try different strategies to determine what works best for you.

Physical:

- Take several deep breaths to gain control of your breathing
- Imagine you are inhaling confidence and exhaling your fears
- Get outside and go for a walk
- Do some gentle stretches and notice how your body feels
- Take a break and have a snack

Mental:

- Notice your anxious thoughts

- Remind yourself that thoughts are only thoughts, not inevitable realities

- Reframe your thoughts into challenges

- Break down the situation into manageable components that you can solve

> Every day is a new opportunity. You can put its failures behind you and start over again. That's the way life is— with a new game every day. We always tell our son James that the best baseball players have the shortest memories!
>
> —Mary Cerbie, Charlotte Latin School
> Physical Educator, Parent of Athletes

Emotional:

- Talk to a friend for support

- Think of someplace happy and safe that stirs up positive feelings

- Watch a funny movie—laughter changes your emotional and physical states

- Do something you know you are good at — creating a positive experience of competence helps counter anxiety

- Do something to help another person—this takes your mind off of your worries and you feel good about helping another

If you find that these strategies do not help you manage your anxiety, talk to your parents or coach. It may be helpful to seek out a professional consultation by speaking to a counselor and/or a medical provider to determine if your experience is performance anxiety or a more significant anxiety disorder.

Overall, remember that mental preparation can help enhance your experience as an athlete. Being mentally prepared is not magical. It does not take the place of physical practice and training, injury prevention/rehabilitation, sound nutrition, adequate sleep, etc. It is a component of the complete athlete—attending to mind, body and emotion.

Far better it is to dare mighty things, to win glorious triumphs, even though checkered by failure ... than to rank with those poor spirits who neither enjoy much nor suffer much, because they live in a grey twilight that knows not victory nor defeat.

—Theodore Roosevelt

7. Managing Stress: The Mind-Body Connection

Stress. We all have it. Even athletes. Schoolwork, family issues, boyfriends, girlfriends, not enough sleep, pressure to make good grades, you name it. It can be positive or negative. However, too much of any stress can seriously affect physical and mental well-being. Athletes may have trouble performing at an optimal level until they have dealt with their chronic stress. We now know much more about the "mind-body connection." It has been estimated that 60% to 70% of all diseases are in some way stress related. Eighty-nine percent of adults report that they experience high stress levels and 75% to 90% of doctor visits are stress related. To achieve total wellness and to be a great athlete we must address all aspects of our lives and strive for balance.

....

Pace yourself. Live to see your success.

—Dennis Waitley

....

What Does Stress Do To Your Body? The "Fight or Flight" Syndrome

Immediate Effects:

• Increased breathing rate

• Increased heart rate and blood pressure

• Fats and sugars are released into your blood stream

• Increased blood clotting

• Increased cortisol (a hormone related to stress)

Long-term Effects:

• Increased cholesterol

• Increased blood pressure

• Increased homocysteine (a measure of inflammation)

• Leads to constricted arteries and abnormal heart rhythms

• Compromised immune system

• Poor memory

• Increased drug abuse and alcoholism

• Increased obesity and overweight

- Stomach and digestive problems

- Grinding teeth, nervous habits

Stress Vulnerability

Recent research has focused on "stress vulnerability." Two people may have the same stressors and problems but one gets sick and one stays well. Why is this? Changing our physical and mental response to the stress can make the difference. Research shows that people who adhere to the following behaviors stay well and develop fewer stress-related diseases. The same things you do to become a better athlete can also protect you from the effects of stress in your life.

- Eat a balanced and nutritious diet

- Exercise regularly

- Get plenty of rest and sleep

- Avoid abuse of alcohol, tobacco, or drugs

- Organize your life and have a plan for your finances

- Surround yourself with positive people and friends you can count on in times of stress

- Take control of situations and make firm commitments to projects you care about

- Nurture your spiritual life

- Laugh often—see the humor in every situation

- Learn to get rid of anger, hostility, and resentment. Get professional help if necessary

- Focus on concerns that have a solution instead of worrying about things you cannot change

- Be assertive and make your needs known to others in an honest and polite manner

- Exercise your brain: read, do puzzles, play games, and visit museums

- Travel and see the world—go on vacation

- Be adventurous—keep the creative spark

- Get a pet—walk a dog whether you own one or not

- Design your castle—your room should reflect the true you and give you serenity

- Volunteer—it takes the focus off of you and it helps others

Sports, Exercise and Stress Management

Exercise is one of the best ways to control and reduce the stress in your life. Activity provides a diversion, getting you away from the source of stress to clear your mind and to sort through the problems. Regular exercise makes you look and feel better about yourself. Others will notice your improved self-concept. Physiological changes that occur with long-term, regular activity provide more strength, endurance, and energy to cope with difficult situations. Muscular tension, which builds up throughout a stressful day, is easily released with aerobic activity and stretching.

These physiological changes are also consistent with disease prevention. Exercise can reverse or improve many of the health problems that are related to stress. Benefits can include decreased blood pressure, lowered cholesterol, reduced stress hormones, and improved sleeping patterns. Other benefits can include improvement in depression and mood, and the lowering of body fat, and lower body weight. When you are in the off-season for your sport or have a long vacation, quickly replace your competitive activity with exercise that you enjoy.

Stress Reduction and Relaxation

Mindful Breathing—a simple deep breath or two can promote an immediate relaxation response. Deep breathing should not happen in your chest but in the abdominal area. Your diaphragm will lower and your abdominals will push out. Take time out for sixty seconds when things get tense. Take time to close your eyes and focus on your breathing.

When your To Do List sneaks into your mind, just go back and focus on your breathing.

Meditation—Follow the instructions for mindful breathing but choose an object or word to focus on. Empty your mind of everything else. Slowly repeat the word mentally, over and over again.

Mental Imagery—During or after the final stretch of your workout or practice, clear your mind and focus on one single image. This could be a shape, a color, your favorite place or anything you associate with quiet and peace. It is simply a "mental vacation." It takes practice to avoid letting your mind wander to other things. Combine this technique with slow, deep breathing.

Visualization—By using mental pictures, you can change attitudes and behaviors. Improve your organizing skills by imagining what your room will look like when it is in order, or improve your posture by imagining puppet strings attached to the top of your head and shoulders.

Progressive Muscle Relaxation—Progressive relaxation trains your muscles to release tension as it builds up instead of storing it throughout the day. Lie in a comfortable position (on your back or on your side with bent knees). Close your eyes. Start by taking several deep, slow breaths. Now, as you breathe in, you are going to tense a muscle or muscle group, and as you exhale let the muscle relax. Focus on how different it feels in the tense state versus the relaxed state.

Follow this sequence:

• Inhale—flex your right foot

• Exhale—let it relax

• Inhale—flex your left foot

• Exhale—let it go

Repeat with the following contractions, inhaling and exhaling slowly each time.

• Flex your feet and tense your calf muscles

• Tighten both legs and press them together

• Tighten the thighs

• Tighten the buttocks

• Pull in the abdominal area and flatten the back

• Tense your chest and shrug the shoulders

• Clench your fists and press your arms into the floor

• Close your eyes tightly and contract your jaw and facial muscles

If you still feel tension in an area, continue contacting and relaxing until the tightness disappears.

• **Massage**—Treat yourself to massage therapy or take turns rubbing your teammates' shoulders after practice. Research demonstrates many valuable health and stress-reducing benefits from massage.

Be good to yourself. This is it! You only get one body and one life. Treat them right. Balance your athletic life, school life, friend life and family life. Other stress-reducing tactics include seeking help when you feel overwhelmed, practicing time management, and finding someone you trust to talk to. Seek opportunities that offer personal growth and discovery. Remember that you are special. Focus on relaxation, enjoyment, and health.

8. Time Management for Busy Student Athletes

You love sports but you also want to do well in school. So here's the scenario. You have just walked in the door from practice. It is 7:30 p.m. and you have not been home since that morning when you left for school. This means you probably have to eat, shower, unpack and repack for the next day, do all your homework, and oh yeah, sleep. Here are some tips to keep the stress level to a minimum.

As soon as you get home, eat something healthy and spend some time with your family. As you will learn in the nutrition chapter, it is important to replace the glycogen in your muscles within 30 minutes after your workout or game. Ignore the rumor that you shouldn't eat anything later in the evening because the truth is your tired body needs to replenish itself no matter what time it is.

> Pressure is nothing more than the
> shadow of great opportunity."
>
> —Michael Johnson

Assess the homework situation and make a plan. Get your priorities straight and work on the hardest assignments or the ones that matter the most first. It is best if you work on your homework in a semi-uncomfortable place—nowhere near a bed, couch, or pillow. You associate all those things with sleep and you will be tempted to go to sleep right away. If you start nodding off or your eyelids feel like they weigh fifty pounds each, it is time to call it a night. Your brain will function better on some sleep even if it's not a lot. So set your alarm for as early as you need to. Just make sure you have enough time to accomplish everything. Maybe set two or three alarms!

When you are at school, make use of little pockets of free time to do your homework for the next day, gather research materials, and get extra help from your teachers. Ask for the next week's assignments on Friday so you can get ahead on the weekends. Make sure your teachers know what your schedule is like so if you look sleepy in class they won't take it personally.

Having a boyfriend or girlfriend is sometimes difficult when you are a serious athlete. You have very little time for dates or talking on the phone. This is one thing your parents will like about your busy schedule!

Take a shower. Use this as a time to plan out how much you have to do and how you are going to get it all done. Make a schedule in your mind while your body is relaxing.

Hint: If you have vocabulary words or something to memorize and if your shower door is clear glass, tape the sheet of paper onto the door from the outside so it is facing in. Your schoolwork won't get wet and you won't fall asleep studying. Plus this is a brand new study spot and will help you learn the material better.

Don't waste time! Turn off your computer so MySpace and Facebook don't use their addictive powers on you. Turn off the sound alarm that tells you when a new email or instant message arrives. This will distract you from your work. Allow yourself 10 minutes to check emails and other computer messages and then resist the urge. Remember the faster you get your work done, the more sleep you get.

If you cannot stop interruptions then go to another room or to the library when you need time alone. Fight for your right to work without distractions.

Divide your To Do List into Urgent and Non-Urgent, or you can use ABC to prioritize. As are things you have to do tonight, Bs would be great to finish but you could also work on them tomorrow, Cs are things you wish you had time to do but they might have to wait for the weekend. You can use colored markers to prioritize items right in your planner while at school.

Break really big projects into smaller chunks of work. Mark the parts of the project off of your list as you finish each one.

Organize your workspace so you can find paper, pencils, note cards, calculator, and reference books quickly and without wasting time.

If you have appointments or breaks in your sports or school schedule, always have reading material or notes to study. Little pockets of time can really add up.

Know yourself. If you know you can't resist looking at your cell phone every two minutes to see your text messages and missed calls—leave it in the laundry room or the garage until your work is finished. If you know you work better after a snack then take time to eat and then get to work. Are you a morning person or a night owl? Do you like to study in groups or by yourself? The more you know about yourself the more efficient and effective you can be.

When your parents see your good grades they will be much more supportive of your athletic commitments.

Passage from "Secrets to Managing My Time"

"The Do-Everything Enigma"

Whenever I'm asked "How do you do it all?" I automatically respond, "I just do," trying to sound humble, while simultaneously brushing away the issue. But the true answer lies much deeper within the academic and athletic jungle, where only truly dedicated and passionate teens survive. First, I sustain an unyielding fervor for all my endeavors, and the lack of such is the primary pitfall for so many young student-athletes. You must be passionate about everything you do, and if this is the case, not only will it be evident in the results and to others, but deep inside on a personal level the activities will be so much more rewarding. Secondly, I am blessed with an unusually vast reserve of energy, thus, allowing the Energizer Bunny inside to keep on going until the weekly full night of sleep. Therefore, when you combine passion and energy—keys to unlocking the "do-everything enigma"—success on some level will come.

But even the zealous, wind-up toy can over-schedule and pay the price academically and athletically. Believe me, I am an advocate for sleep, and for knowing your own limitations, and this means prioritizing. What can you really do in 24 hours? I am an organizational madman, planning exactly how each day will go, given the unavoidable vicissitudes of reality, and following through on that plan to the "T." This requires an immense amount of willpower, and as I said, prioritizing—should I go to the movie at the detriment to my math grade? Or, make poor decisions as to what I put into my body at the expense of my athletic performance? So love what you do, rest when you can, and balance by prioritizing.

—*Greg M., Age 17, High School Junior, Varsity Football and Baseball Player, Student-Athlete Committed to Community Service*

Spend your precious time on things that truly are important and can make a difference. Good grades, becoming a better athlete, getting enough sleep, and spending time with your family or a friend are all worthwhile and will have a lasting benefit. Watching TV, instant messaging and surfing the Internet may have to wait!

9. Fruits and Veggies Reduce Oxidative Stress

A fter a long practice or game you feel tired but good. Although you are working hard and getting stronger and more flexible there is also something going on inside your cells. The very oxygen that you breathe is attacking your cells. Chemical reactions in your body produce oxidants, which are called free radicals. These free radicals are missing an electron, which makes them very unstable. They run around your body trying to "steal" an electron from your healthy molecules. This can cause damage to cell membranes, red blood cells, muscle fibers, proteins and even your DNA (your blueprint to make more cells).

| NORMAL OXYGEN ATOM | LOSS OF ELECTRON | FREE RADICAL |

You produce billions of free radicals per day, per cell in your body. They are missing an electron so they are unstable and can cause damage to healthy molecules in your body. Athletes produce more free radicals than other people. Your food choices will help you stop these free radicals in their tracks before damage occurs.

The free radicals cause a chain reaction of destruction to your cells. By attacking cell membranes, they cause cellular damage, muscle fatigue, injury and vulnerability to chronic disease. Everyone experiences oxidative stress but athletes and people who exercise strenuously have excessive amounts. As intensity and duration increase— oxidative damage increases. So while exercise and sports activities are good for you, you need to prevent long-term damage by eating the right foods (antioxidants and phytonutrients) to stabilize and stop the free radical damage.

Some diseases linked by research to oxidative stress:

Cardiovascular disease *Alzheimer's disease*
Cancer *Parkinson's disease*
Lung disease *Cataracts*
Macular degeneration (eyes) *Poor immune system*
Diabetes *Wrinkling and skin damage*
Arthritis

**Other factors in the production of
free radicals and oxidative stress:**

Alcohol consumption *Psychological stress*
UV light from the sun *Toxins in the environment*
Smoking or second hand smoke *Sickness and injury*

How to Eat the Right Foods to Get Antioxidants and Phytonutrients

There are thousands of nutrients and live enzymes in fruits, vegetables, nuts, seeds, beans, and grains. These are called "phytochemicals" or "phytonutrients." We will call them phytos for short. There are different ones in each color of fruits and vegetables. So broccoli has different phytos than sweet potatoes or blueberries. These phytos have all the antioxidants you need to neutralize the free radicals and stop damage to your body. Both the best research and our government recommend 9 to 13 raw fruits and vegetables be included in your diet every day. This is what it takes to prevent disease, prevent damage to your proteins, and build your immune system. Isolated, man-made vitamins have not been found to be effective in lowering oxidative stress except in higher toxic doses, e.g. side effects like kidney damage. You must get antioxidants from your food. Each color of fruits and vegetables has different nutrients, and they all have important roles in human nutrition and in maintaining health. One apple has over ten thousand identified phytos. These nutrients work in a delicate balance to perform all of the important functions in the cells of your body. You cannot get this from a man-made vitamin pill. If you know you don't eat the recommended amount every day, try a whole food supplement that is actually made from real juiced fruits and vegetables. See the next chapter and the Recommended Resources for information on Juice Plus+® which is the product I recommend to my clients. Choose fruits and vegetables with a lot of color: dark green, purple and blue, deep orange and red and don't forget the nuts, seeds and whole-grains.

Athletes Should Eat the Rainbow Every Day!

According to the government's New Food Guide Pyramid, teenage athletes need thirteen different colors of raw fruits and veggies every single day.

Blue and Purple—Great at Stopping Those Free Radicals!

Blackberries

Blueberries

Black currants

Dried plums

Elderberries

Purple figs

Purple grapes

Plums

Raisins

Purple asparagus

Purple cabbage

Purple carrots

Eggplant

Purple Belgian endive

Purple peppers

Potatoes (purple fleshed)

Black salsify

Go for the Green!—Lowers risk of cancer, protects your vision, and builds strong bones and teeth.

Avocados

Green apples

Green grapes

Honeydew

Kiwi

Limes

Green pears

Artichokes

Arugula

Asparagus

Broccoflower

Broccoli

Broccoli rabe

Brussels sprouts

Chinese cabbage

Green beans

Green cabbage

Celery

Chayote squash

Cucumbers

Endive

Leafy greens

Leeks

Lettuce

Green onion

Okra

Peas

Green pepper

Snow Peas

Sugar snap peas

Spinach

Watercress

Zucchini

WHITE is Right!—Good for your heart and lowers cancer risk.

Bananas
Brown pears
Dates
White nectarines
White peaches
Cauliflower
Garlic
Ginger
Jerusalem artichoke

Jicama
Kohlrabi
Mushrooms
Onions
Parsnips
Potatoes (white fleshed)
Shallots
Turnips
White Corn

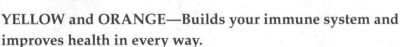

YELLOW and ORANGE—Builds your immune system and improves health in every way.

Yellow apples
Apricots
Cantaloupe
Cape gooseberries
Yellow figs
Grapefruit
Golden kiwi
Lemon

Mangoes
Nectarines
Oranges
Papayas
Peaches
Yellow pears
Persimmons
Pineapples

Tangerines
Yellow watermelon
Yellow beets
Butternut squash
Carrots
Yellow peppers
Yellow potatoes
Pumpkin

Rutabagas
Yellow summer squash
Sweet corn
Sweet potatoes
Yellow tomatoes
Yellow winter squash

I SAID RED—Helps you remember things, prevents urinary tract problems, and protects your heart.

Red apples
Blood oranges
Cherries
Cranberries
Red grapes
Pink/Red grapefruit
Red pears
Pomegranates
Raspberries
Strawberries

Watermelon
Beets
Red peppers
Radishes
Radicchio
Red onions
Red potatoes
Rhubarb
Tomatoes

10 Ways Athletes Can Eat More Fruits and Veggies:

1. Pack dried fruit like raisins, apricots, and figs in small bags with raw almonds in your gym bag.

2. Make a fruit or chocolate banana smoothie for breakfast or after practice.

> When dealing with the pressures of training and competition, it is important to know there are many variables that affect performance, such as genetics, development, and emotional maturity. Yet nutrition is a major component that is too often overlooked for its benefits of providing energy and chemical protection for optimal performance.
>
> —Paul Stricker, MD, FAAP, Sports Medicine Pediatrician, Olympic Physician, From his book *Sports Success Rx!*

3. Cut up veggies and make a healthy dip on the weekend so you can grab-and-go all week!

4. Keep a big bowl of apples, pears, and oranges on the counter to throw in your lunch or your gym bag for school or practice. No packaging required!

5. Always eat fruit on your cereal (whole-grain is best).

6. Order sides of veggies in restaurants. Almost all restaurants will bring you a side of broccoli (skip the cheese sauce) or green beans.

7. See how colorful you can make your salad. Try for at least five different colors of veggies. Croutons and Bacon Bits® don't count!

> Athletes are often undernourished, although many of them eat lots of food. They often engage in eating patterns that may provide short-term benefits, but are unhealthy in the long-term. Fortunately, it is possible to enhance sports performance while building, not destroying health.
>
> —Pamela A. Popper, PhD, ND from *The Wellness Forum's Guide to Sports Nutrition*

8. Learn to eat food with beans. Put beans on your salad. Rice and beans and Mexican dishes are delicious!

9. Try 100% fruit juice instead of soda or other sugary drinks. Orange juice with calcium and vitamin D is a great choice but the real fruit is even better because it has the fiber intact.

10. Fresh pineapple has an enzyme that repairs muscle—a great snack after a hard class or rehearsal.

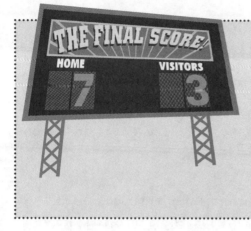

Healthy eating and stopping oxidative stress is all about color and phytonutrients from fruits and vegetables. Your Plate Should Look Like a Rainbow!

10. Whole Food Nutrition for Athletes and Their Families

The right diet can enhance your performance as an athlete and as a student and can help you lead a long and happy life. The real news is not that a healthy diet is good for you —we all know that—the real news is that a healthy diet may save your life. From the last chapter we now know that consuming a variety of the right foods lowers a person's risk for many chronic diseases and enhances the benefits gained through regular exercise and sports training. Sport-specific

> Your caloric intake is directly linked to performance, recovery, normal growth and development, and body weight goals. The young athlete has nutritional requirements that are greater than average people. These requirements can be met by eating 5 to 7 small, nutrient-dense meals throughout the day. Make sure you follow a sports-specific nutrition program, consume enough calories, and get adequate periods of rest and recovery. Remember, NO PAIN, NO GAIN and TRAIN UNTIL YOU DROP is for fools.
>
> —From *PowerPack for the Winning Edge,* by Jack A. Medina, MA and Roy E. Vartabedian, PhD

workouts and exercise sessions, combined with proper nutrition, will aid in weight control, help reduce calcium loss from bones, and reduce the negative effects of stress and anxiety. No matter what your personal goals for sports may be, a nutrition plan is essential.

It can be difficult to make these changes when most of your friends are feasting on fast food and pizza. It takes discipline and planning to eat an optimal diet day in and day out. The good news is that the same dietary changes that make you a better athlete will also build your immune system and protect you from illness and disease. A few carefully made changes can modify your nutritional habits for a lifetime of optimal health and maximal performance.

What Should I Eat?

All individuals should consume a plant-based diet with about 65% to 70% of calories from carbohydrates, 15% of calories from protein and 15% to 20% from fat. Athletes simply need more calories than the average person because of their activity level. The proportion of each nutrient in the diet remains the same, so the entire family can make these changes together. The research is very clear that the same dietary choices that prevent cancer and heart disease also reduce your risk of obesity, eye disease, Alzheimer's, Parkinson's and many other lifestyle-related diseases. The changes are not all easy but they are simple. If your favorite food is high in fat and sugar you will need to save it for very special occasions or perhaps decrease the quantity. If you really savor the taste you may not need such a large portion. Go for quality—not quantity!

The information in this book is intended as a general guideline for the athlete and the rest of the family. If you have any medical conditions or are taking any medications it is important to consult a registered dietitian and your physician for specific advice.

Carbohydrates

Carbohydrates are the most important nutrient for exercising muscles and are needed for optimal brain and central nervous system function. The recommended amount of carbohydrate for athletes is 65% to 70% of your total caloric intake. Carbohydrates are necessary nutrients but it is important to consume the right kind. Refined sugars and starches like white bread, sodas, cookies, donuts, and candy have little nutritional value and are quickly absorbed and stored as fat. Because these sugary foods are digested so quickly they overload the blood with glucose.

Complex carbohydrates are foods that are left in their whole state such as whole-grains, fruits, vegetables, and legumes (beans). They still have the vitamins, minerals and fiber intact and they take much longer to be broken down. Their sugars are released much more slowly into the bloodstream avoiding excess glucose in the blood.

How Sugar Harms: Ten Good Reasons for an Athlete to Avoid Simple Sugars

1. Sugar can suppress the immune system.

2. Sugar can cause difficulty with concentration and promote hyperactivity and anxiety.

3. Sugar can upset the mineral balance in the body.

4. Sugar can produce a rise in your triglycerides and a decrease in your good cholesterol.

5. Sugar can feed cancer growth.

6. Sugar contributes to the reduction in defenses against bacterial infections.

7. Too much sugar can lead to a chromium deficiency.

8 Sugar can increase fasting levels of glucose.

9. Sugar can cause hypoglycemia.

10. Sugar can produce an acidic digestive tract.

Fiber

Eating a lot of complex carbohydrates will automatically give you enough fiber. Fiber refers to the components of plant cell walls that are not digested by human intestinal enzymes. It is also called "roughage" or "bulk." When whole-grains are processed or refined, much of the fiber is removed and many of the nutrients are lost. Fiber adds bulk to the diet, absorbs water in the intestine and produces larger, softer stools that are easily eliminated. This decreases the time that cancer-causing agents are in contact with the lining of the large intestine and colon. This also inhibits the absorption of toxins into the bloodstream. People who consume a high-fiber diet have less colon cancer, heart disease, cholesterol problems, and gallstones. Soluble fiber forms a gel as it moves through the digestive system interfering with the absorption of cholesterol. Oat bran, oatmeal, barley, rice bran, apples, oranges, strawberries, prunes, carrots, corn, broccoli, lentils, navy beans and pinto beans all contain soluble fiber. Fiber of any kind is also great for weight loss and weight control as it fills the stomach and decreases appetite. Conditions associated with low-fiber diets are chronic constipation, diverticulitis, irritable bowel syndrome, Crohn's disease, colitis, and blood clots in veins and lungs. Cancer, heart disease, diabetes, and kidney problems have all been linked to low-fiber diets.

The optimal diet should have about 45 grams of fiber a day. Fruits, vegetables, legumes (beans), nuts, whole-grain breads, cereals and rice are great choices. You can build up to this amount slowly so your digestive system will have time to adapt.

Protein

Protein's job is to build and repair body tissues, including muscles, tendons, and ligaments. It is also necessary for the synthesis of hormones, enzymes, and antibodies, as well as fluid transport and energy. In developed nations, especially the United States, it is very rare for insufficient protein intake to be a problem. Most of us eat too much, especially animal protein, and choose poor quality sources. Research suggests an active adult needs about 15% of their calories to be comprised of protein. Excess protein puts stress on the digestive tract, kidneys, and liver. Too much protein from animal sources causes an excess of uric acid in the bloodstream. Uric acid is a by-product of protein metabolism. In order to neutralize this acid the body steals calcium from bones and other stores in the body, leeching the body of calcium. Some nutritionists and researchers believe the reason we need such a high intake of calcium is because of our extremely high intake of animal protein. Some even implicate the rise in osteoporosis with the increase of animal protein in our diets. The Nutrition Committee of the Council on Nutrition, Physical Activity, and Metabolism of the American Heart Association states, "High-protein diets are not recommended because they restrict healthful foods that provide essential nutrients and do not provide the variety of foods needed to adequately meet nutritional needs. Individuals who follow these diets are therefore at risk for compromised vitamin and mineral intake, as well as potential cardiac, renal, bone, and liver abnormalities overall."

Can athletes be vegetarians? Will they grow and perform just as well on plant foods? Yes. You can easily get the protein you need from fruits, vegetables, soy foods, beans, grains, seeds, and nuts. Research is showing that by keeping your animal food consumption to fewer than 10% of your total calories that you will help prevent disease as you get older. This means you don't have to be a complete vegetarian but you have to move in that direction to protect your health. Only consume protein supplements and energy bars made from plant protein such as soy-based smoothie mixes (see Recommended Resources). Research indicates that if you can keep your intake of animal foods to less than 10% of your caloric intake, your risk of disease goes down dramatically. This means you can get excellent protein from plant sources for many of your meals. Nuts, seeds, grains, beans, and soy products all contain high-quality protein. If you choose to eat beef and poultry choose organic, low-fat varieties and do not consume the skin. Free-range and grass-fed are best. Free-range eggs are a better choice as they have a higher ratio of omega-3 fatty acids. Purchase organic animal foods if you can, to reduce your consumption of steroids, antibiotics, growth hormone residues, etc. Think of animal foods as a small condiment-sized serving instead of the main part of your plate.

Protein is not what builds muscle. Training is what builds muscle. Eating a balanced, 90% plant-based diet will give your body the building blocks it needs to do its thing. With the right choices, athletes can perform at a high level and still protect themselves from developing diseases in the future.

Fat

Fat is the primary fuel you use for light to moderate-intensity exercise. You should not consume more than 15% to 20% of your calories from fat. The essential fatty acids provided by the fat in your diet are important for maintaining healthy cell membranes, healthy skin, making hormones, and for transporting certain vitamins. The type of fat is the important thing. It is best to get your fat from food and not added oils.

Reduce Saturated Fat and Cholesterol

Animal food is the primary source for saturated fat in the diet. Fat on beef, pork, veal, the skin on poultry, dairy products like cheese, milk, lard, and butter, are all common sources of saturated fats. It is also found in palm oil, palm kernel oil, and coconut oil. There is overwhelming research showing that diets high in saturated fats raise the risk of heart disease, stroke, and many forms of cancer. One of the hardest foods to restrict is cheese. Cheese is very high in saturated fat and is included in almost everything we eat.

Avoid Trans-Fat or Hydrogenated Fat

These are fats that have been altered to make food products have a longer shelf life. They are very damaging and are mostly found in cookies, cakes, crackers, fast food, and other highly processed foods. Trans fatty acids are very hard for your body to break down. They stick together causing fatty deposits in the arteries and the liver. Like saturated fat, they are associated with a higher incidence of heart disease and stroke and depress the immune system. If the label says a food has trans fats—put it back. There are plenty of other choices without it.

The Good Fats

If you choose to consume oils, the best choices are monounsaturated fats like olive oil and canola oil. Good fats come from nuts, seeds, flax seeds, avocados, and olives. Remember that all oils are equally high in calories. It is best to get your fat calories from foods and not added oils. Carry a bag of raw almonds and walnuts mixed with dried fruit in your sports bag, add avocado and a few nuts to your salad, and put ground flax seeds into your smoothie.

Omega-3 Fatty Acids

Every cell in our body needs omega-3 fatty acids to function optimally. We cannot manufacture them ourselves so they must be ingested. The omega-6 fatty acids are also essential but our modern diets contain plenty of this oil. During the last century people in developed countries like the United States have eliminated almost all omega-3 fatty acids from their diet. Where we used to have a ratio of one omega-6 to one omega-3 we now have a ratio of 20 omega-6s to one omega-3 in our diets.

What do omega-3 fatty acids do in the body? They help control energy production in the cell and they are the building blocks of your cell membranes, controlling what comes in and out of the cell. Research has discovered that this depletion of omega-3s has had a very negative effect on our bodies, particularly on the brain and the heart. The rise in heart disease and depression has directly paralleled this decrease in omega-3 consumption. Other diseases related to this deficiency are rheumatoid arthritis, diabetes, postpartum depression, cancer, obesity, asthma, attention disorders, and aggression/hostility in teenagers.

There used to be an abundance of omega-3 fatty acids in the food supply especially in populations that ate fish and wild game. When cows and chickens were allowed to roam free and eat grass, the meat and eggs had a much higher content of omega-3s. Because our food supply has changed drastically people consume little or no omega-3s. Salmon that is farm-raised have no chance to eat the algae that makes wild, fatty fish high in this essential nutrient. Fish have also been contaminated with environmental pollutants like mercury and PCBs, which makes it less desirable to eat the amounts needed to get adequate omega-3s.

How to Get More Omega-3s:

Increase omega-3 fatty acids in your diet and decrease omega-6-containing oils (corn oil, safflower oil and sunflower oil).

Good sources of omega-3s are:

- Flax and hemp seeds (grind whole seeds in your coffee grinder)
- Walnuts
- Soy foods/tofu
- Oily fish (salmon, mackerel, tuna)
- Fortified eggs or eggs from free-range/grass fed chickens
- Wild game

• High-quality/purified fish oil supplements although these are still risky because they can oxidize or spoil and can have contaminants. Many nutrition professionals no longer recommend consuming oil of any kind. (See Recommended Resources for more information and check with your registered dietitian or physician before consuming a supplement.)

What is Your pH? Acid versus Alkaline Diets

Research is showing that people who eat a more alkaline diet are healthier. Cancer cells and most diseases thrive in acidosis. Our body is able to heal itself if we provide a more alkaline environment. This means eating about 80% plant-based foods (fruits and vegetables) and about 20 percent acid foods (proteins like meat, fish, milk, eggs, and poultry as well as fats, grains, and sugars). This is the opposite of the typical American diet which focuses more on acidic foods. If you have eggs and bacon for breakfast, turkey and cheese for lunch and pasta and meatballs for dinner you are consuming a mostly acid diet.

Do Athletes Need Supplements? Whole Food versus Man-Made

Researchers are beginning to understand that vitamin supplements cannot make up for a poor diet and that isolated supplements rarely show any ability to prevent disease. In several studies, isolated, man-made supplements were found to cause more harm than good. If you think about this it makes sense. Our bodies need thousands of nutrients, so eating the whole food item works better than pulling out one nutrient and hoping that it will work by itself. We simply need to eat food in the way it was put on earth: whole and unprocessed.

Athletes need to ingest sufficient energy to meet the physical demands of their intense and oftentimes lengthy training sessions. Consuming the right amounts and types of food and fluid will provide their body with the fuel needed to achieve optimal training benefits and peak performance.

—Tina Marie Mendieta MS, RD/LDN

The government and researchers have spent billions of dollars and many decades trying to find a cure for heart disease, cancer and other diseases. They have tried to discover what is the one thing in the orange that is good for you. After years of study we now know that it is the synergy of the whole orange that allows your body to function at its very best. Food should be eaten in the proportion in which it was put on earth, not in fragmented, isolated vitamins or man-made elements. There is overwhelming evidence that people who eat a variety of raw fruits, raw vegetables and unrefined grains have the least amount of disease.

The problem is that very few humans actually consume the necessary amount and variety of these healthy foods. Sometimes a carefully chosen supplement can bridge the gap in your diet.

Guidelines for Choosing a Supplement:

This section is excerpted from *PowerPack for the Winning Edge* by Roy Vartabedian, PhD and Jack Medina, MA. See the Recommended Resources at the end of this book.

1. Are you sure the product does not contain any harmful or "extra" ingredients? Just because it is natural does not mean it is safe. Recently, popular children's vitamins were found to contain lead.

2. Does the supplement contain whole foods from real fruits, vegetables, and grains, or is it made of isolated, man-made vitamins?

3. Does it contain ingredients that have no proven benefit? Testimonials may be abundant, but there is no real gold standard, peer-reviewed, published research showing that the supplement is actually absorbed and has benefits in the body.

4. Was the research done on the actual product and not a selected generic ingredient? Does the research show

benefits in the human body (not rats)? Is there a placebo group (where one group gets the real thing and the other gets a sugar pill)? Is it a double-blind study, in which nobody knows who got the product and who got the placebo, until the study is over? Is it published in a peer-reviewed scientific journal (real and independent science)?

5. Does the company that makes the supplement make fantastic or unbelievable claims about their product? Do they use famous people or professional athletes with testimonials? Words like "miracle," "cure," "amazing," "secret formula," and testimonials about diseases that were cured should raise red flags. Only prescription drugs may claim to treat or cure diseases, not supplements.

Whole Food Supplements

People know they should eat more fruits and vegetables but in reality it is not happening. If you know you do not eat 9 to 13 fruits and vegetables each day, the best insurance is a whole food supplement. This is especially important in athletes because of the extra oxidative stress and free radical damage from training so hard. I recommend one to my clients called Juice Plus+®. Taking Juice Plus+® capsules every day provides the nutritional foundation we so desperately need and that is so lacking in our diets today. Juice Plus+®

is not a vitamin supplement providing a limited number of handpicked nutrients. Juice Plus+® is a whole-food based product providing the wide array of nutrients found in a variety of nutritious fruits, vegetables, and grains. It's the next best thing to fruits and vegetables because we don't get nearly enough of the real thing every day. Juice Plus+® comes in capsules, chewables, and gummies. It is certified as gluten-free and is kosher. This is one of the very few supplements that I recommend because it has a large body of primary, peer-reviewed research to show that it improves immune function, improves circulation, lowers inflammation, and reduces oxidative stress in normal people and in athletes. Juice Plus+® has been analyzed to determine what's in it, where it goes in the body, and what it does when it gets there. This is very rare in the supplement world. Juice Plus+® is the perfect answer for those of us who try hard in our busy lives but don't always get the recommended 9 to 13 fruits and veggies into our systems every day. See the Recommended Resources for ordering information.

Protecting the Athlete's Bones

Bones are living tissues, constantly being remodeled and reacting to hormonal changes, nutrition, and stressors applied to them. Osteoporosis is a disease in which low bone mass and deterioration of bone structure causes bones to be weak, porous, brittle, and susceptible to fracture. At highest risk are Asian and Caucasian females who are relatively thin and sedentary, postmenopausal women without estrogen support, and those with a family history of osteoporosis. Black females are at lower risk possibly because of greater bone mass. Men can develop osteoporosis but it usually shows up much later in life. Researchers are beginning to realize that the main cause of osteoporosis is a high intake of acidic food, mainly animal protein. The higher the intake of protein, the more uric acid is produced which must be neutralized by calcium from bones and teeth. Animal products and processed foods contain high levels of phosphorous which also has to be neutralized with calcium. Osteoporosis is linked with kidney disorders because of the high stress on the kidneys to eliminate the leftovers from protein metabolism. The answer is to eat a diet high in fruits and vegetables, which have a high calcium-to-phosphorous ratio. Plant-based calcium is much more available and easy to absorb and it prevents the leeching of calcium from bones and teeth. Try to increase tofu, soy products (processed with calcium sulphate or calcium chloride), raw almonds, calcium fortified orange juice, bok choy, broccoli, kale, turnip greens, parsley, mustard greens, and endive. Calcium is not effective without vitamin D, so consume foods fortified with added vitamin D like orange juice, soy milk, and cereals. Other foods with vitamin D include egg yolks, salmon, and sardines. Exposure to sunshine for 10 to 15 minutes without sunscreen allows your body to make its own vitamin D. Never stay out long enough to burn.

What About Dairy Foods?

The only drink that is biologically necessary after weaning
is water. Recent research is finding that dairy products
may not be the health food that we once thought they were.
For one thing, the pasteurized, homogenized milk that we
drink is very different than the raw form people drank
in the past. Dairy foods are a huge source of saturated
fat. Whole milk is 49% fat and 2% milk derives 35% of its
calories from fat. Most cheeses are about 70% fat. Saturated
fat is linked to insulin resistance, higher cholesterol, heart
disease, and stroke. Dairy sugar is called lactose. About 55%
of the calories in fat-free milk actually come from this sugar.
Many people are lactose intolerant, which can cause severe
stomach upset. The protein in dairy foods has come under
scrutiny for contributing to type 1 diabetes, loss of kidney
function in diabetics, prostate cancer, and ovarian cancer.
Migraine sufferers and people with rheumatoid arthritis may
find that dairy protein is a trigger for attacks. Cow's milk is
high in phosphorous, which can combine with calcium and
can prevent you from absorbing the calcium in milk. Milk
protein also accelerates calcium excretion from the blood
through the kidneys. This is also true when you eat large
amounts of meat and poultry products. Vegetarians will
need about 50% less calcium than meat eaters because they
lose much less calcium in their urine. If you consume less
animal protein in general you will actually need less calcium

because your diet is more alkaline than acid. Most people consume dairy for the calcium but it is very easy to get calcium from plant foods. You would be surprised how great organic soy milk, rice milk, and almond milk taste. Most of these come in vanilla, chocolate, and strawberry flavors. Look for products that are not genetically modified. They will be labeled as non-GM.

Avoid These to Prevent Osteoporosis:

- Tobacco—Lowers hormone levels, thereby accelerating bone loss. Stopping smoking at any age slows bone loss.

- High caffeine intake—Increases the amount of calcium excreted in the urine, depriving the bones of calcium they need. Carbonated sodas have phosphates, which cause loss of calcium from bones and teeth.

- Alcohol consumption—Suppresses bone tissue formation.

- Excessive dieting—Hurts the bones by depriving the body of important nutrients, including calcium. Eating disorders can also affect bone health.

- Excessive physical activity—Can cause bone loss by depressing hormone levels, evident when a female athlete begins to miss her normal menstrual periods (amenorrhea).

Strategies for Preventing Osteoporosis

- Consume a calcium-rich diet—calcium is essential to healthy bones. This is extremely important during the teen years and early adulthood when we build our peak bone density, but also throughout our lives. Vegetable, nut and fish sources are best, including almonds, calcium-fortified juice, tofu, soy products (processed with calcium sulphate or calcium chloride), bok choy, broccoli, kale, turnip greens, canned sardines, salmon with bones, Juice Plus+ Complete® smoothie, or calcium supplements as needed. It is best to get your calcium from food sources.

- Vitamin D—Necessary for our bodies to absorb calcium. Good sources are sunshine, fortified foods like orange juice, soy milk, rice milk, and cereals. Also include salmon, sardines, egg yolks, and Toni's Smoothie (Recipe in Chapter 11).

- Weight Bearing Exercise—Running or jogging are perfect. Most sports involve weight-bearing exercise, except swimming and cycling. Just be sure to add some strength training for the arms and upper body. Research shows this is very important for maintaining bone health.

- Consult a physician or registered dietitian—learn about your risk for osteoporosis and the recommended treatment.

Eat a "whole-food" diet that is mostly plants in a rainbow of colors. Consume healthy fats and proteins. Avoid chemicals and additives in "processed" foods. Athletes need more calories than non-athletes but they should still be "healthy" calories.

These findings show that heart disease, diabetes and obesity can be reversed by a healthy diet. Other research shows that various cancers, autoimmune diseases, bone health, kidney health, vision and brain disorders in old age (like cognitive dysfunction and Alzheimer's) are convincingly influenced by diet. Most importantly, the diet that has time and again been shown to reverse and/or prevent these diseases is the same whole foods, plant-based diet that I had found to promote optimal healthy in my laboratory research and in the China Study. The findings are consistent.

—T. Colin Campbell, PhD excerpted from *The China Study*

11. What Do I Eat? Practical Guide

Carbohydrates like cereal, pasta, bread, rice, vegetables, and fruits are the main fuel for training and competition. Glycogen in the liver and in muscles needs to be replaced by carbohydrates in the diet. Failure to recover glycogen stores leads to early fatigue, lower exercise intensity, and increased risk for illness and injury.

What to eat before practice:

What you eat the three days before is more important than the night before. A diet that is only 50% carbohydrate will eventually lead to a decline of glycogen in your muscles and liver. An athlete's diet should be at least 60% to 70% carbohydrate to maintain energy stores. The closer you eat to the time of heavy activity, the smaller the meal should be. A heavy meal could lead to cramping and low energy. Your muscles are competing with your digestive system for blood flow and energy. Good pre-game choices include fruit, vegetables, pasta, baked potato, healthy snack bars, whole-grain toast or English muffins with spreadable fruit. Poor choices include animal protein and high-fat foods such as chicken nuggets and fries or a steak dinner, that are slower to digest and can make you sluggish during your activity.

What to eat after practice or after the game:

Within 30 minutes of a hard training session (or as soon as possible) consume a meal or snack containing about 80% carbohydrate and 20% protein. A peanut or almond butter and fruit spread sandwich, raw almonds and dried fruit, beans and rice, pasta and veggies, or a fruit and plant protein smoothie (recipe on page 120) would be great.

What to eat during a competition or a long tournament:

Drink water between each game or activity session and take small bites to keep your energy up. Orange, kiwi, or apple slices, a banana, a couple of raisins, plain bread or a bagel would all work. Do not consume anything with a high fat or protein content or a drink with a high sugar content.

Meal and Snack Ideas for Athletes in Training:

• Cereal (whole-grain with soy or rice milk) with fruit

• Whole grain sandwich with hummus, spreadable fruit and peanut or almond butter, veggies, organic turkey

• Brown or wild rice with veggies or beans

- Whole-grain tortilla wrap with veggies, beans and avocados

- Pita pocket with veggies, tuna, salmon, or hummus

- Whole grain pasta with veggies and/or tomato sauce

- Fruit of any kind (fresh pineapple has an enzyme that repairs muscle)

- Baked potato or sweet potato

- Oatmeal

- Raw almonds, pecans, or walnuts mixed with dried fruit

- Parfait with fruit and granola

- Celery and peanut or almond butter

- Raw veggies with hummus or a low-fat dip

- Baked tortilla chips with salsa

- Graham crackers or gingersnaps dipped in applesauce

- Mini rice cakes with peanut butter

- Healthy sports bars/granola bars are preferable to fast food or vending machines (try Kashi® brand or a bar with low sugar, high-fiber, and a plant-based protein source)

- Homemade banana bread, corn bread, or muffins

- Juice Plus+ Complete® smoothie with fruit (recipe on page 120)

Healthy Recipes

Toni's Smoothie Recipe for Athletes (and Tired Parents)

This can be altered to fit your taste buds. It is a complete meal replacement, quick and healthy breakfast or after-training snack to reload muscle glycogen. This provides over half your days worth of calcium—all from plant sources. I have found that a good blender makes all the difference. My kids like it to be smooth! Play around with it until you find a combination that you love.

French Vanilla Smoothie with Fruit
Blend until smooth
> *1 cup of vanilla soy milk, plain soy milk, almond milk, rice milk, water, or calcium fortified juice*
> *1 scoop of French Vanilla Juice Plus+ Complete® (see Recommended Resources to order)*
> *1 ripe banana*
> *1 Tablespoon brewer's yeast or nutritional yeast (provides B vitamins, an important addition for vegetarians)*
> *1 Tablespoon ground flax seed for Omega 3s (just put whole seeds in your coffee grinder)*
> *Frozen or fresh fruit*
> *I like to use a few strawberries, peaches, raspberries, blackberries, and blueberries*
> *Ice (optional but makes it thicker and colder)*

Chocolate Banana Smoothie

Blend until smooth

1 cup of vanilla soy milk, plain soy milk, rice milk,
almond milk, or water

1 scoop of Dutch Chocolate Juice Plus+ Complete®
(see Recommended Resources to order)

1 ripe banana

1 Tablespoon brewer's yeast or nutritional yeast

1 Tablespoon ground flax seed for Omega 3s (just put
whole seeds in your coffee grinder)

1 cup of ice

Jenna's Favorite Parfait

Start with a pretty, long-stemmed glass and layer the
following ingredients. You can make it the night before if you
prefer granola that is not too crunchy. Top it with a whole
strawberry or a design of berries. Pick a pattern and then
repeat.

Strawberries, blueberries, blackberries, or pineapple
(any fresh or thawed frozen fruit will work)

Granola (organic if possible)

Organic yogurt or non-dairy yogurt

Dried dates or raisins

Wrap-Ups to Go

This is a great way to get several veggies in at once. Easy to pack and carry. Put it next to a cold or frozen water bottle to keep it cool for several hours.

Whole-wheat tortillas or flatbread

Filling: choice of hummus, black or kidney beans, organic turkey, wild salmon, or other healthy choice

Shredded carrots, purple cabbage, cucumbers, spinach, sprouts, red peppers, corn or any other veggies

Healthy salad dressing (optional)

Sports Bag Trail Mix

(Place in a small zip-lock snack bag/make enough for the whole week)

5 or 6 raw almonds

5 or 6 raw walnuts

3 Brazil nuts

¼ cup dried apricots

¼ cup dried plums

Pieces of healthy cereal or granola (about 8 pieces)

Tips for Eating Out and Choosing Wisely:

- Choose foods that are broiled instead of fried, such as a grilled chicken sandwich instead of fried chicken or chicken nuggets, grilled fish instead of fried fish, etc.

- Choose soups that are broth or tomato-based and not cream based.

- Choose a tomato-based sauce instead of Alfredo or cream sauce for pasta. If they have whole-wheat pasta, ask for this as a substitute.

- Always ask for your salad dressing on the side. Have low-fat salad dressings instead of the full-fat kind. Romaine, leaf lettuce or spinach are much more nutritious than iceberg lettuce.

- Always substitute another side dish for French fries. Most restaurants will bring you broccoli or the veggie of the day. Some offer fruit or a salad as a choice. Baked potatoes or sweet potatoes without the butter or sour cream (or with a tiny amount) are better than fries.

- Use mustard or ketchup instead of mayonnaise.

- When ordering a sub or sandwich, select the veggie choice or leaner meats like turkey or grilled chicken. Stay away from fried items like burgers or steak and cheese sandwiches.

- Choose water instead of sodas, fruit drinks, and milkshakes.

- When ordering pizza, add lots of veggies instead of meat. Ask for half the cheese or no cheese.

- When ordering Chinese or Asian food, ask for no MSG (this is a chemical preservative and taste enhancer) and ask that veggies be steamed with the sauce on the side to decrease the fat. Avoid fried foods. Ask for brown rice if available.

- If fruit and veggies are available, try to add them into your meal. For example, have lettuce and tomato on sandwiches or burgers.

At lower intensities, the body is pretty good at burning fat from the aerobic system, which is the most efficient fuel it can burn. When intensity increases, your body relies more on the anaerobic system and burns more "sugar." Since this form of fuel is stored in the body in limited supply, you can exhaust your storehouse if you work out too hard, too fast and/or too often. Repeating this pattern is what sets many people up for over-training injuries and sickness apart from the fact that it is exactly what can result in uncontrollable food cravings, preventing many from reaching their ultimate fitness goals! The trick is to balance training from a variety of intensities based upon your unique metabolic make-up. Using heart rate-based training is an excellent way to exact which fuel system an individual relies on at varying levels of intensity. The next step is to allow for proper recovery which speaks to proper nutrition and adequate levels of rest!

—Kyle Radaker, MS, Owner of Custom Cardio and Fitness

Some Ideas for Popular Restaurants:

Burger King®, Fuddruckers®, and Backyard Burger®, as well as other restaurants offer a veggie burger. You owe it to yourself to be brave and try it with lettuce, tomato, onion, ketchup and mustard.

At our local Mexican restaurant I have them make a naked burrito in a bowl with cilantro rice, black beans and pinto beans. Heap on the chunky salsa and lots of lettuce. This is a delicious vegetarian meal with plenty of plant-based protein.

At Italian restaurants, (Macaroni Grill® and Nothing but Noodles® are the ones we have) I order whole wheat pasta with marinara sauce. I add broccoli, carrots, sun dried tomatoes and mushrooms. Delicious! Some of my best meals have been when I ask the waiter for a plate of their best vegetables. The chefs seem to really like this and they send a beautiful plate every time!

A broth or tomato-based soup with bread is always a good choice.

Almost every restaurant has a grilled or blackened salmon choice. Ask for vegetables and a baked potato to eat with it.

If You Have to Eat Fast Food:

You can check out your favorite fast food place or restaurant on the Internet. You can find the company Web site by doing a Google search. Once you have found the Web site, look for the "nutrition section." There is usually a link on the home page to the nutrition section where you will find nutrition facts, including fat, cholesterol, sodium, protein, calories, and more. This will help you make better choices when eating out. Here are a few examples of poor choices and somewhat better choices when you have to eat fast food. You will see that even the "better" choices have huge amounts of sodium and very few nutrients. Look for mostly vegetable salads, fruit, baked potatoes, or veggie burgers at many restaurants. Try to limit fast food to once a week at the most.

McDonalds® Poor Choices

Small Fries (250 calories; 13 grams fat; 140 mg sodium)
Large Fries (570 calories; 30 grams fat; 330 mg sodium)
Quarter Pounder with Cheese (510 calories; 26 grams fat;
    1190 mg sodium)
Nuggets 6 Pack (250 calories; 15 grams fat; 670 mg sodium)
Strawberry Triple-Thick Shake (1110 calories; 27 grams fat;
    130 mg sodium)

McDonalds® Better Choices

Fruit and Yogurt Parfait (180 calories; 2 grams fat;
    85 mg sodium)

Southwest Salad with Grilled Chicken (320 calories; 9 grams fat;
970 mg sodium)

Chic-fil-A® Poor Choices
Chicken Biscuit (420 calories; 19 grams fat; 1270 mg sodium)
Chicken Sandwich (410 calories; 16 grams fat; 1300 mg sodium)

Better Choices at Chic-fil-A®
Char-grilled Sandwich (ask for lettuce and tomato; 270 calories;
3.5 grams fat; 940 mg sodium)
Char-grilled Salad (This is without dressing/choose low fat or
non-fat; 180 calories; 6 grams fat; 620 mg sodium)

Taco Bell® Poor Choices
Grilled Beef Burrito (680 calories; 30 grams fat; 2120 mg sodium)
Fiesta Taco Salad (840 calories; 45 gra,s fat; 1780 mg sodium
(without shell 470 calories; 25 grams fat; 1510mg sodium)

Taco Bell® Better Choices
Crunchy Tacos (150 calories; 8 grams fat; 370 mg sodium)
Grilled Steak Soft Shell (160 calories; 4.5 grams fat; 550 mg sodium)
Spicy Chicken Soft Taco (170 calories; 6g fat; 580 mg sodium)

Wendy's® Poor Choices
Big Bacon Classic Sandwich (590 calories; 30 grams fat;
1510 mg sodium)
Chicken Club Sandwich (650 calories; 31 grams fat; 1580 mg sodium)
Medium Chocolate Frosty (430 calories; 55g sugar)

Wendy's® Better Choices

Sour Cream and Chives Baked Potato (320 calories; 4 grams fat; 55 mg sodium)

Mandarin Chicken Salad (170 calories; 2 grams fat; 480 mg sodium; add dressing: 190 calories)

Caesar Chicken Salad (90 calories; 5 grams fat; 620 mg sodium; add dressing: 120 calories)

Burger King® Poor Choices

Double Whopper w/cheese (990 calories; 64 grams fat; 1520 mg sodium)

Spicy Chicken Sandwich (720 calories; 36 grams fat; 2000 mg sodium)

Onion Rings—Large (450 calories; 22 grams fat; 660 mg sodium)

Burger King® Better Choices

Chicken Garden Salad (240 calories; 9g fat; 720 mg sodium; add light Italian dressing: 120 calories; 11g fat; 440 mg sodium)

Chicken Tenders—5 pc. (210 calories; 12g fat; 600 mg sodium)

Grocery Shopping—Be a Smart Consumer

- Try to buy foods that contain ingredients you recognize or would use at home.

- Stay on the perimeter of the grocery store. This is where the fresh, whole food is sold.

- Avoid products containing the following ingredients: trans fats, partially hydrogenated oils, artificial sweeteners (aspartame or Splenda®), MSG, nitrites, nitrates, artificial colors, sulfites, potassium bromate, and brominated vegetable oil.

- The following terms all mean one thing—sugar! Brown sugar, honey, dextrose, maltose, lactose, fructose, rock sugar, and corn syrup and high-fructose corn syrup—these are all terms for the same thing. No one sugar is healthier or better than another, they are all simply empty calories and replace healthier choices. High sugar in your diet will depress your immune system and compromise your health.

- Check serving sizes. Most of us eat much more than a typical serving. A small bag of chips might actually be 2½ servings. This is a sneaky trick! You must multiply the calories and fat by the number of servings, or by 2.5 in this case, to get your total nutritional intake.

What is a serving size?

It is more important to eat a variety of fruits and vegetables of many colors than to worry about the exact serving size. Most foods are ½ cup per serving. Loose foods like lettuce are one cup and dried fruit and nuts (denser foods) are ¼ cup. Athletes often need more calories than less active people but the extra servings should still come from healthy sources.

Foods That Drain the Body and Brain

White bread, white sugar, alcohol, artificial sweeteners, artificial food colorings, colas, frostings, corn syrup, nitrate and nitrate-containing foods, high sugar drinks, candy, nicotine, processed snacks, fast food with high fat and sodium, and any foods with a long list of ingredients you don't recognize as real foods.

Super Foods for Serious Athletes— Choose Some to Eat Every Day

Nutrition-packed food choices that will improve your performance and help to prevent illness now and when you are older! Research is showing that these foods truly can make a difference:

wild salmon, beans, walnuts, avocados, Brazil nuts, spinach, blueberries, sweet potatoes, broccoli, cinnamon, garlic, collard greens, kale, brown rice, bananas, kiwi, soy, oranges, onions, dried fruit (apricots, figs, plums, raisins, dates, cranberries), tomatoes, black and green tea, and pumpkin.

THE FINAL SCORE

HOME 7 VISITORS 3

Eating well takes planning and self-control. What you eat day after day is more important to your performance than what you eat right before you compete. Enlist your entire family so you can make healthy changes together. Be a role model for good nutrition on your team.

Many popular sports drinks are high in sugar and lack many nutrients, making them essentially empty calories. The body does not hydrate efficiently with substances other than water, which should be the first-choice beverage for an athlete. Electrolytes, which are found in many sports drinks, are easily obtained with the proper diet.

—Pamela A. Popper, PhD, ND
From *The Wellness Forum's Guide to Sports Nutrition*

12. Drink, Drink and Be Healthy

Everyone, including athletes, should drink 6 to 8 glasses (8-ounces) of water each day. Children should consume half of their weight in ounces. A 50-lb child would need 25 ounces per day. Adequate fluid intake is necessary to replace fluids lost through metabolism, daily activity, sports, and other vigorous exercise. The amount lost depends on many factors including environmental temperature, humidity, and your ability to dissipate heat. When you are dehydrated, even just a little, studies have shown your energy level will drop as well as your ability to focus. Every system in your body depends on water to work properly. Cooler water is absorbed faster than warm or room temperature fluids. Drink water before, during, and after your practice. Foods like bananas, pineapples, oranges, and kiwis will help maintain the electrolytes that you need for long workouts. Sports drinks with a high sugar content can cause cramping and are not recommended. A drink like Propel®, with a tiny bit of carbohydrate, may improve taste and help athletes consume more fluid. You can also add lemons, limes, or a little cranberry or grape juice to water to improve the taste. For extreme endurance events, drinks containing electrolytes and carbohydrate are sometimes needed but for a normal practice or game water is usually the best choice.

Guidelines for Exercise Fluid Replacement:

- Consume 8 to 16 ounces of fluid at least one hour before the start of practice or the game.

- Consume 4 to 8 ounces of fluid every 10 to 15 minutes during the workout.

- Consume 16 to 24 ounces during the 30 minutes after exercise even if you do not feel thirsty.

- For serious athletes it is a good idea to weigh yourself before and after practice to monitor your fluid loss.

What's the Big Deal About Soft Drinks?

- Athletes (and their families) have no reason to consume regular or diet sodas. They can only hurt performance and decrease health. At most, sodas should be an occasional treat. There are many reasons to avoid soft drinks:

- High sugar content (23 grams for 8 ounces, which is about 6 teaspoons for every 8 ounces)

- They contain no nutrients (we call this "empty or liquid calories")

- High phosphorous, which depletes calcium from bones and teeth

- They replace healthy choices like water

- Diet drinks have aspartame and Splenda® (chemicals)
- Many contain caffeine (addictive, depletes bones)

Ten Ways to Add More Water to Your Day:

1. Always carry a bottle of water with you in the car. Drink on the way to your destination and on the way home.

2. Ice it down! Cold water tastes better.

3. Set a goal. For adults, fill two 3-ounce containers in the morning and make it a goal to finish them before bedtime. Young athletes should drink half their weight in ounces of water.

4. Ask your teachers if you can keep a bottle of water on your desk at school to sip all day. Your brain is 85% water and cannot function or focus without proper hydration.

5. Drink with a straw. It goes down faster and easier.

6. Squeeze in lemon, lime, or orange juice to add a bit of flavor.

7. Humans sometimes mistake thirst for hunger. When you are hungry start with a glass of water.

8. Eat fruits and vegetables that contain a lot of water, such as watermelon, oranges, celery, carrots, and lettuce.

9. Next time you start to order a soda, stop and get water with lemon. You have just saved yourself ten teaspoons of sugar or more. Your body will thank you.

10. Be a role model at practice and at games. Make sure all the other kids see you drink water instead of sodas or sugary drinks.

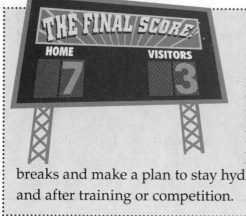

Water is necessary for every function in your body. Humans have a faulty thirst mechanism so you have to take purposeful water breaks and make a plan to stay hydrated before, during, and after training or competition.

13. Body Image and Disordered Eating

—with Charee Boulter, PhD, Psychologist

Adolescence is a time when many changes are happening to your body. As you mature your body begins to transform from the body of child to a more adult body. During this time questions about your appearance are common. There is considerable pressure to have the "right look" that is promoted in magazines, on TV and in the movies.

....

It wasn't until I lost a match to someone ranked 200 places below me that I realized that I had no more energy left. I turned on the television one day, and there was a show on about eating disorders. I saw myself in the people on the show and decided it was time to do something about my eating disorder and the stress that was dominating my life.

—Zina Garrison, Tennis Player, Two-Time
Olympic Medalist, Federated Cup Captain

....

Although Zina is a female athlete, eating disorders are also becoming increasingly more evident in males. Guys, please don't skip this chapter—you may help save a life.

For an athlete the awareness of physical changes in appearance and in the body's ability to adapt to these changes can be heightened. How your body feels during different movements changes. Athletic maneuvers that once were easy may be more difficult during a growth spurt. Because athletes have more muscle, you might weigh more than your friends who are the same size. On the other hand you may find that you are thinner than your athletic peers and worry that you are not strong enough. As an athlete you may find that your awareness of these physical changes is amplified, because you spend several hours per week exercising with your teammates.

Athletes are at increased risk of developing concerns about their body image and, therefore, eating disorders. Coaches and others may assume that lower body fat is positively related to increased performance. Popular sports magazines commonly have weight loss articles. An athlete who over-trains may be rewarded for his/her dedication. Sports that involve monitored weigh-ins place athletes at an increased risk, such as wrestling, crew, and horse racing. Sports that involve subjective judging also place athletes at increased risk, including figure skating, gymnastics and diving. Additionally, increased public awareness of the use of "performance enhancing" drugs and supplements (some illegal) by professional athletes, has sent messages about the lengths some individuals will go to in their attempt to win.

Individual feelings of self-doubt and self-consciousness can lead an athlete to criticize his or her body. Comments from your coach on body position, which are intended to help you improve your form and skills, can sound harsh and critical. On a day when you are feeling low, comments such as "use your legs, jump higher," may sound like criticisms of your body; thus, "use your legs, jump higher," may become interpreted as "my legs are too short" or "my legs are too soft and weak."

If you are concerned that you or a friend may be struggling with body image concerns what should you do? How do you know if it is a body image issue or the common self-doubts of adolescence? Check the lists below to help you determine if it is a body image issue and what to do.

Signs of body image dissatisfaction:

- Frequently makes negative comments about one's self.

- Avoids shopping for clothes with others (especially trying on clothes in common dressing rooms).

- Frequently asks about one's appearance—"Does this look OK?"

- Has frequent "bad hair" days.

- Moods are connected to feelings about appearance and/or weight.

- Makes comments about the appearance of others—both positive and negative.

- Compares self to others—"She is so pretty and I'm not. Her life is perfect."

- Thoughts and worries about appearance interfere with daily activities.

- It is difficult to concentrate and stay focused during practice or competition.

- Getting dressed takes too long due to multiple clothing changes.

What to say to a friend struggling with body image issues:

- Make positive comments about her personality and talents.

- If she makes negative self-comments, tell her that you feel sad when she says such things about herself.

- Reassure her that she is beautiful inside and out.

- Avoid making comments about your own physical appearance and others'.

- Make an effort to focus on the strengths and functions of the body rather than the appearance of one's body.

Sometimes when an athlete struggles with body image concerns she may begin to diet and/or use supplements

In an attempt to change her body shape. It is important
to remember that healthy nutrition is key to optimal
functioning. Diets often eliminate crucial nutrients and/or
adequate calories, placing an athlete at risk for a variety
of physical problems, e.g. exhaustion, weakness, stress
fractures, etc. Weight loss or muscle-building supplements
can contain harmful ingredients. When diets go awry,
disordered eating can be the result.

An eating disorder is complex and is much more than a
body image disturbance combined with an out-of-control
diet. There are many factors related to the development
of an eating disorder. An athlete is not "crazy" if she
develops an eating disorder. In fact some of the personal
attributes that help an athlete excel can also place her at
risk of developing an eating disorder; such as, being high
achieving, goal-directed, and paying attention to detail.
Some athletes may appear confident but may actually
struggle with low self-esteem. Some may have a family
history of eating disorders or other mental health disorders
that place them at increased risk.

An eating disorder can have significant negative effects
on one's health. The most serious is death. In 1994, Christy
Henrich, a gymnast, died due to health complications related
to an eating disorder. Problems that may be of heightened
concern for athletes include:

- Fatigue

- Dizziness

- Decreased ability to concentrate

- Increased overuse injuries

- Stress fractures

- Decreased cardiac functioning (increased risk of heart failure)

- Weakened immune system

It is important to know the common signs of an eating disorder. If you recognize these signs in yourself or a friend, please talk to a trusted adult and seek professional assistance:

- Noticeable weight changes in a short period of time

- Excessive dieting, even after achieving original goal

- Belief that one is fat even though she is not

- Belief that one is too skinny or weak even though she is not

- Changes in eating patterns, such as eating alone, eating limited types of food

- Avoiding social events where food is served

- Uncontrolled binge eating

- Use of dieting, purging, exercise or medications to compensate for overeating

- Mood is dependent upon weight

- Loss of menstrual period

> My eating habits were a mess. For six or seven years, I was bulimic. A lot of that was my attitude that I would do anything to win…it was no one's fault but mine — my perfectionism, my need to win.
>
> —Megan Neyer, Eight Time NCAA Champion Diver

Help is available for athletes struggling with disordered eating. Comprehensive treatment usually involves medical care, individual and group therapy, and nutritional therapy. A treatment team, which may include a physician, a therapist, and a dietitian, is often developed to address the athlete holistically. In some cases the coach may be included in some aspects of this treatment team. For example, if the athlete needs to take some time away from training during recovery. Family therapy may be a component of treatment. In most cases outpatient treatment is sufficient. Some individuals may need more intensive care and thus may spend time in a hospital or inpatient treatment center.

If you suspect that a friend is struggling with an eating disorder express your concerns to her. She may be embarrassed and try to hide her disorder, so do not worry if she does not seem happy that you are expressing your concern.

- Find a time when you are not likely to be interrupted.

- Use "I" messages to identify your concern and avoid accusing her of having a problem.

- "I am worried about you."

- Tell her what you are worried about.

- Identify specific concerns such as: noticeable changes in eating patterns, physical fatigue, negative body image, etc.

- "I have noticed you seem really tired and you have been dieting. I am concerned that you might have an eating disorder."

- Be a good listener.

- She might open up and share her struggles with you.

- She might deny having a problem.

- You can be a good friend and listen.

- Be understanding.

- Remember that having an eating disorder does not make a person crazy.

- You can probably relate to some of her feelings and concerns, but to a lesser degree.

- Ask her to see a professional.

Treatment for an eating disorder can be lengthy. Sometimes an athlete may begin to make improvements by addressing the underlying issues—family issues, depressed mood, low self-esteem—before the eating behaviors improve. Be patient. The end result of successful treatment is worth it.

You cannot fix eating disorders yourself. Get professional help or recommend help for your friend.

Players don't get better from drills or practice. Those things reinforce talent. Players get better from game time experience. They learn how to react, to strategize, to set goals and to deliver when they are in the heat of a game. A great coach will let that happen. Very little gain comes from riding the bench. Except maybe a good dose of humility.

—Mary Yorke Oates, High School and Collegiate Athlete, Basketball and Field Hockey Coach, Former US Olympic Development Coach

14. Outside Training Programs and Camps

Summer camps and intensive sports programs are excellent ways to improve your skills, become more versatile, and learn from great coaches and former athletes. This is a chance to build your skills without the stress of competition. You may get more "game time" at a camp than you do during your season on your regular team. You may attend these programs with your team or a group of friends or you may sign up and go as an individual. Some are on weekends and some are entire weeks during the summer or holiday vacations. Some summer camps require a personal invitation either by a recommendation from your coach, by trying out in person or by sending in a video of yourself. If your goal is to compete at the high school, collegiate, or professional level, special camps are a great way to buff up your skills and be seen by the people who matter.

If you are not getting playing time reach deep for more determination. Hard work and extra practice will help you overcome your weaknesses. There is always someone out there working harder than you. Even if you are good you can always be better.

—Will L. , Age 17, Student, Basketball Player

How to pack for a camp:

Food and Drinks:

• Water bottle or cooler of drinks (sometimes you have only a few seconds for water breaks so don't waste them waiting in line at the water fountain or the water table).

Lots of "10-second snacks"

• Baggies of whole-grain cereal with dried fruit

• Fruit of any kind–orange slices, apples–remember fresh pineapple has an enzyme that repairs muscle

• Raw almonds and walnuts mixed with dried fruit

• Healthy sports bars/granola bars are preferable to fast food or vending machines (try Kashi® brand or a bar with low sugar, high-fiber, and a plant-based protein source)

• Homemade banana bread or muffins

• Whole-grain bagel with peanut butter

Ideas for packing lunch for camp:

• Sandwich with hummus, spreadable fruit and peanut or almond butter, organic turkey

• Tortilla wrap with veggies, beans and avocados

- Pita pocket with veggies, tuna, hummus, etc.

- Fruit, bananas, cut up kiwi, orange slices, or fresh pineapple

Other Things You'll Want to Remember:

- First aid items such as band-aids, toe tape, ankle or knee brace if you use one

- Toiletries and hair supplies: deodorant, hairbrush, hairspray, ponytail holders, barrettes

- An extra pair of shoes—or at least laces in case one breaks

- Socks—switch to dry socks halfway through each day for better foot care

Camp Etiquette

- Don't be late! Start out each session on a good foot. Be on time with all your equipment ready to go. Try not to yawn while the coaches are talking. Even if you are going on your 5th hour of camp and suffering from a severe case of sleep deprivation, try to resist the urge. If you absolutely have to yawn or cough make sure you cover your mouth.

- Don't chew gum! Enough said.

- Be courteous to other athletes. This is a great chance to develop camaraderie but still give your all in drills and play. Play hard but fair.

- Be respectful to the coaches and instructors. Do not get in the front row if you do not know the drill or exercise. Don't ever sit down or cross your arms. Always make sure you thank the coach at the end of each session.

 Attending summer camps and special coaching clinics in addition to your regular practices is one of the best ways to push yourself to the next level and become a stronger and more versatile athlete.

15. Surviving and Thriving as a Sports Family

My heroes are and were my parents. I can't
see having anyone else as my heroes.

—Michael Jordan

From the Father of an Athlete

Being the father of an athlete means more than just sitting in the stands of a gym or playing field waiting for your child's turn to play. Fortunately for us, the expectations for you as the dad of an athlete are not too high but there are basic rules you must understand and follow. Obviously, the rules will differ slightly depending on whether your child is playing recreational lacrosse or AAU basketball. Hopefully you will discover this after only one or two events. The obvious ones, like arrive early and wear comfortable clothes, are similar to what you would find in any college entrance exam prep book. This chapter will prepare you for the many other rules that require more experience and preparation. So don't be nervous.

Arrive early because you will have to be sure your athlete has time to get mentally prepared and physically warmed up. This will take more time than you think. Nothing bothered me more as a coach than having a couple of players wandering in to the locker room just as I completed presenting a thorough game plan and a rousing pre-game pep talk. You will also have other family members with you who will be working as a team to get the best seats possible. Since there are no reserved seats and saving seats is frowned upon, their mission is critical. You may have to count on your group to save you a seat while you go find a place to park the car and hike all the way back to the stands.

Make sure you wear your team's color somewhere on your body—or at least some team's color or logo. You definitely want to at least look like a former athlete. Certainly your team and child would prefer you be there wearing anything, but if possible, can you at least change out of the surgical scrubs or the business suit before you take the field? Bring a noisemaker, like an empty plastic water bottle with a few small rocks or beads slipped inside. And definitely locate a copy of the team roster or program or you will be lost. Knowing which players wear which numbers and who is on what team certainly adds to your enjoyment of the sport. If you have to visit the men's room or the concession stand and you miss his great play, definitely don't admit to it. Nothing could be worse. So smile, rattle your noisemaker, give him a hug, and tell him he looked great out there. Maybe he won't find out.

Choose your seat quickly and with confidence—team parents can be a competitive bunch. They will detect any hesitation on your part as a sign of weakness. Plus you probably make a better door than you do a window so sit down quickly to avoid blocking others' view of the game. Your group should have selected seats in an area with other parents from your team, hopefully a row or two behind the bench and as close to the action as possible. Doing so will allow you to experience the event and see the excitement through your child's eyes and will definitely make it more fun.

Don't boo the players competing against your child. As much as you might want to turn this into a professional hockey game, positive support is better. Since players may be influenced by the loudness of crowd noises, a noiseless clap for the competition is best. No reason to help out the other team, right? But it is okay to yell and clap loudly when your team or child does something well —the louder the better. The kids really do perform better if they sense excitement from the spectators. Generally any sounds you might have made at a wrestling match or NASCAR event would do well here.

Enjoy the concessions. Many of the competition venues have an excellent selection of sandwiches, ice cream and specialty drinks but they have few healthy choices so if you are inclined to eat when you're bored, be careful. Consider having a nearby pizza store deliver a large order to share but you may have to eat it on the steps because some places absolutely do not allow outside food to be brought into the arena. I have found a six-inch sub sandwich slips nicely into a coat pocket and if you go easy on the onions no one will ever know.

Bring a survival kit. Lacrosse teams play in the rain, football teams battle in the snow, and baseball teams compete in the heat. Although games are usually canceled for hurricanes, don't count on it. You will need to bring a few things:

- A blanket and seat cushion—stadium seating is not for the skinny. To fight the cold and bed sores, a little cushioning helps.

- An umbrella or piece of plastic—some places do not allow umbrellas lest you drip all over the person seated next to you, but a large cut of polyethylene folds nicely in your pocket and can serve as a tent for the serious storms.

- Folding chair. These are great for relaxing in on the sideline so count yourself lucky if you remember to bring yours.

- A towel or plastic bag—for your kid's muddy cleats.

- Sunglasses with polarized filters—you really will see the action better with less glare and protect your peepers from ultraviolet light damage.

- Cash. Your experience as a human ATM will come in handy here.

Forget about sneaking away for golf or to a nearby sports bar to catch the semifinals of the NCAA basketball tournament. This is March Madness of a different sort. Competition Softball Leagues, Swim Team, Travel Team Soccer, and AAU Basketball are tremendous time commitments with various events scheduled throughout the day. Just to see all of your child's games may require over five and half hours of sitting in your seat. If you add in time spent watching other teams or athletes worth seeing compete, it leaves very little time for anything else.

Get an experienced parent to explain the game rules to you. They can be complicated, especially if your child is involved in a sport you never played before. Lacrosse, for example, a typically northern sport, had not made it south when I was in school but it is now huge in our area. Understanding the rules required me to buy and read a primer on the sport, which at times read like the IRS tax code. Doing this little bit of homework allowed me to familiarize myself with the rules, strategies, and various basic moves for my child's sport. Only then will you understand that when Andrew scored a goal after a flag was dropped that it really did count. Only then will you appreciate that Will's stick is longer because he is a defender. And you will be able to yell "offsides!" with confidence and appreciate that when Taylor drove the field to kick a winning goal or Ginny won the game by acing her serve, it truly was amazing.

Practice the *Rudy* philosophy. Years ago there was a football movie about a kid with little ability but lots of heart who stuck with his dream to play college football for Notre Dame. This true story, a movie called *Rudy*, helped me teach my child the best attitude to have when he was not getting the playing time he thought he deserved. I urged him, and players I have coached, to do what you can to help the team. Be positive, supportive of your teammates, work hard every day in practice and your time will come. Then I made him watch the movie. Also, as a parent, don't bad mouth the coach in front of your child or give support to his complaints about how bad the officiating was. Those too-easy targets are seldom the reasons for a bad outcome, and giving in to that sets a bad example for your child.

As a father of an athlete your number one role is support. Get involved. Be an assistant coach. Take pictures of everyone's kids. Put together a first aid kit and become the one the kids come to for a bandage or ice pack. You can be confident that the money you spend on sports is being put to good use. The sports world is teaching your child life skills and confidence. These athletes train and practice because they want to do well. They put their hearts into each event. With these rules and a little effort you will survive and thrive at their practices, games, and competitions. And just you being there will make all the difference in the world.

Notes from a Sports Mom:

The best part of allowing your children to participate in athletics is the chance you have to watch them mature, gain new skills, and grow as people. The healthy atmosphere, the social time with friends, and the chance to contribute to a team effort are just some of the benefits. Whether your child is the "star" or the "chief bench warmer," your job is to show up, be there before and after the game and make sure that all experiences turn into an eventual positive one.

Here are some practical "Mom" tips that may save you from learning things the hard way:

- Have a family meeting to decide how much time and money can be devoted to athletics and how many sports each child can play. Some sports can be very affordable and others require extensive resources. This will also depend on how well your child can juggle sports and school, how many siblings are also participating in activities, and how much travel is required for a particular sport.

- Help your child come up with a system to get the uniform clean and to keep all equipment and shoes ready and waiting for the next practice or game. This is a huge source of stress if you are late and cannot find the things you need.

- Drive to and from practice and games with your athlete as much as possible. We have amazing conversations on these car rides. Conversations shift from explaining the game strategy and rules to deeper important discussions about life.

- Try to eat healthy as a family, exercise, and manage stress in a proactive way. Keep the pantry and refrigerator stocked with lots of fruits and vegetables and whole-grain snacks. Find time to take care of yourself. You must be a good role model for your athlete. Studies show the number one predictor of whether your children will grow up and have healthy habits is whether you model this for them.

- Most of all have fun and treasure every moment.

Younger Brother and Sister Survival Guide

—by Will Branner

Ten Ways to Entertain Yourself at a Game or a Three-Day Tournament

If you are under 12 years old:

• Bring action figures and toy cars.

• Make a fort out of the folding chairs and your parent's blankets.

• Draw people with funny faces and mustaches on the program or stat sheet.

• Bring a football or Frisbee to throw on the next field with the other kids.

• Eat something from the concession stand every hour or bring healthy snacks (get money from Mom or Dad)

• Bring your Game Boy.

• Bring your portable DVD player to watch a movie.

• Take a nap.

• Watch your sister or brother play.

• Tell her/him how great she/he did!

If you are over 12 years old:

• Bring an iPod or another way to listen to your own music.

• Meet girls and kids from other teams and schools.

• Bring homework and get ahead for the coming week.

• Bring your portable gaming system (remember to charge it before you leave home).

• Meet more girls.

• Take a nap.

• Actually watch most of the game or match. You will be impressed.

• If you can't beat them—join them! After years of watching my sister, I now play football, lacrosse, and basketball.

16. Lessons for Life from Sports

—by a Young Athlete

Here are some things that I have learned through athletics that I believe will help me in life:

Dedication—If you are serious about sports, you commit your body, your mind, your time, and your energy to it. I have learned to devote my life to something I truly care about.

Confidence—To play and compete in front of your peers, family and community takes courage and will. This self-assurance will help me take new opportunities in the future without hesitation and will keep me from holding back.

Time Management—I have learned to make use of time. If I have homework or something to do I get it done efficiently because the faster it gets done, the more sleep I get.

Passion—For me, sports are something that I can turn to for support. I can express myself without having to explain anything. It is an escape for me when everything else is going wrong. Once you have found a passion it becomes a base that you can always return to even if you are 45 years old and CEO of a company.

Perseverance—Sometimes on the last set of push-ups, sit-ups, or sprints you are not sure if you can do any more.

Sound familiar? Participating in sports has taught me to push myself farther than I ever thought possible. I now know that when I reach a point in life when most people would just give up, I can continue to fight and push myself to my limit.

Here are some words from my favorite coach of all time, the venerable John Wooden of UCLA who captured 11 NCAA Men's Basketball Championships. In his mid-90s, Coach Wooden still serves as an inspiration to millions of basketball fans around the world. One of the things I most admire about Coach Wooden is that the principles he followed to become the most successful college basketball coach in NCAA history, could be applied to life in every vocation. He is an amazing man.

Five Things a Leader Should Keep in Mind
from Coach John Wooden:

1. Adversity thins the ranks of your competition.

2. Getting individuals to mesh their goals
with team goals is your goal.

3. Worthwhile objectives take time, which
requires patience, and which requires faith that
things will work our as they should.

4. You are imperfect; so is everyone else.

5. Meticulous planning is meaningless without hard work.

—Arch McIntosh, Headmaster, Charlotte Latin School

Sacrifice—In order to train and do well in school I have had to sacrifice many things. The amount of sleep I get, my social life with school friends, and being involved in multiple activities such as my school's musical or playing another sport are all affected by my commitment to one sport. But that is a decision I have made and I am okay with it. In fact it is a true test of how far you are willing to go and how much you are willing to sacrifice. You might want to play several sports or you might want to play one and focus on that one sport year round. Think seriously about your goal and then arrange your schedule so you can achieve that goal. Being able to prioritize your life is an important life skill.

I want all of my students involved in our school sports program. One of the primary components of athletics for students is to provide them with healthy social interactions in a positive peer group. Kids will find a peer group—I want to be sure that that group has a healthy focus and is led by good role models. I am proud that we also promote "winning with class" and "losing with dignity"—great life lessons to foster resilience and good character.

—Debbie Lamm, Head of the Middle School at
Charlotte Latin School (Also a Former Bench Warmer
on a High School Championship Volleyball Team)

Leadership—One of the best ways to get better at your sport is to watch those who are older and have more experience than you. I learned so much from watching these older role models and now that I am the oldest, I can be a role model myself. Choose a team and sports program where the coaches are people you can look up to as well. Sometimes you are with them more hours than you are with your own parents. Your coaches and fellow athletes become part of your family and you benefit from these relationships. Respecting and learning from my role models has taught me how to be a leader.

It could be drama, sports, music, or horseback riding, but it is important for everyone to find something they are passionate about. That dedication and commitment will teach and reinforce many skills needed for a happy and healthy life. A few of us might actually become professional athletes. That is great but probably won't last forever. You will still need all of these life skills to deal with your success in a positive way.

About the Author

Toni Branner is director of Fitness Concepts, Inc., and teaches on topics such as anti-aging, children's wellness, motivation for lifestyle change, whole food nutrition, stress management and safe exercise.

Toni received her Master's Degree in Exercise Physiology from the University of North Carolina at Chapel Hill where she also served as director of the UNC Employee Health and Fitness Center and as a faculty member in the Department of Physical Education, Exercise and Sports Science.

Branner has authored two previous books. *The Safe Exercise Handbook (5th Edition)* promotes the importance of a regular exercise program as a means of improving your health and quality of life. This book is used on US Navy aircraft carriers to guide military personnel through their workouts. *Wilby's Fitness Book,* includes innovative ideas to help children stay healthy and feel good about themselves.

Through fitness classes for children and adults, as well as numerous speaking engagements, workshops and academic presentations, Toni has shown thousands of people the way to perform effective, injury-free fitness and achieve maximal health.

Recommended Resources

The Care & Feeding of an Athlete resource list is available at:
www.thecareandfeedingof.us

Up-to-date lists of camps, equipment, books, magazines, Web site links, private coaches, and more.

Also new recipes, training methods, and updates on any new research that would interest athletes.

Author Information:
Toni Tickel Branner, MA
Exercise Physiologist, Wellness Consultant, Physical Educator, Professional Speaker

Professional Speaking, Workshops, and Seminars on Fitness, Nutrition and Stress Management

The Care & Feeding of an Athlete Seminars for Parents and Athletes

The Care & Feeding of an Athlete Free E-Updates

The Care & Feeding of a Dancer Studio Seminar for Parents and Students

The Care & Feeding of a Dancer Free E-Updates

Health Made Simple Free E-Updates for people interested in general health, fitness and nutrition

Contact Toni at Fitness Concepts

Website: *www.tonibranner.com*
Email: *tonibranner@aol.com*
Phone: (704) 551-9051

Books and Resources by Toni T. Branner, MA

The Care & Feeding of an Athlete by Toni T. Branner

The Care & Feeding of a Dancer by Toni T. Branner

The Care & Feeding of a Soccer Player by Toni T. Branner

Wilby's Fitness Book by Toni T. Branner

The Safe Exercise Handbook and Workout DVD with upper body and lower body exercise bands by Toni T. Branner (*www.tonibranner.com*)

Recommended Books for Athletes and Parents

Sports Success Rx! by Paul R. Stricker, MD (*www.aap.org/parenting books*)

Dr. Sears' LEAN Kids
by William Sears, MD and Peter Sears, MD

PowerPack for the Winning Edge
by Roy Vartabedian, PhD and Jack Medina, MA

The China Study by T. Colin Campbell

Prevent and Reverse Heart Disease
by Caldwell B. Esselstyn Jr., MD

Eat More, Weigh Less by Dean Ornish, MD

The Omega-3 Connection by Andrew L. Stoll, MD

Digestive Tune-Up by John A. McDougall, MD

Dr. Neal Barnard's Program for Reversing Diabetes by Neal D. Barnard, MD

Hungry for Health by Susan Silberstein, PhD

Recommended Web sites and Newsletters

Paul Stricker M.D. Website *www.drpaulstricker.com*

American Council on Exercise *www.acefitness.org*

American Heart Association *www.americanheart.org*

American Dietetic Association *www.eatright.org*

American College of Sports Medicine *www.acsm.org*

American College of Cardiology *www.acc.org*

American Cancer Society *www.cancer.org*

Fruit and Veggie Info and Recipes *www.5aday.com*

Center for Advancement in Cancer Education *www.beatcancer.org*

Nutrition information unbiased by industry *www.pcrm.org*

The Wellness Forum *www.wellnessforum.com*

Dept. of Agriculture site for families and children *www.mypyramid.gov*

Fruit and Veggie Info and Recipes *www.vegweb.com*

Bill Sears, MD Wellness Website *www.askdrsears.com*

Product Recommendations

Fitness Equipment

For fairly priced, high quality fitness equipment, weights, mats, stability balls, videos, etc.

Fitness Wholesale: (888) FWO-RDER or *fitnesswholesale.com*

For Juice Plus+* Whole Food Nutrition Products

Juice Plus+® provides the nutritional essence of 17 different fruits, vegetables, and grains in convenient and inexpensive capsule form.

For information and research

Go to: *www.juiceplus.com* or call (800) 347-6350

(Children between the ages of 6 and 15 years are eligible to take Juice Plus+®+® for free for up to three years as part of the Children's Health Study if one adult takes the capsules.)

For Juice Plus+ Complete® Smoothie Mix

We recommend this product because it is plant-based protein and is perfect for breakfast or for replacing glycogen in the muscles after games or practice. It is high in calcium, vitamin D, phytonutrients and fiber.

Comes in French Vanilla, Dutch Chocolate, and Variety Pack

Go to: *www.juiceplus.com* or call (800) 347-6350

For hundreds of resources for athletes, or to sign up for free E-Updates go to:

www.thecareandfeedingof.us

Please contact me with feedback and comments on the material in this book. I would love to hear from you and visit your team or school sometime. The best to you and your family and keep playing!

—Sincerely, Toni Branner